LABOR
IN SOVIET
GLOBAL
STRATEGY

LABOR IN SOVIET GLOBAL STRATEGY

ROY GODSON

Preface by Irving Brown

Crane Russak · New York
National Strategy Information Center, Inc.

Labor in Soviet Global Strategy

Published in the United States by

Crane, Russak & Company, Inc.
3 East 44th Street
New York, NY 10017

Copyright © 1984 National Strategy Information Center, Inc.
150 East 58th Street
New York, NY 10155

Library of Congress Cataloging in Publication Data

Godson, Roy, 1942-
Labor in Soviet global strategy.

(NSIC strategy paper series; 40)
Rev. ed. of: The Kremlin and labor. c. 1977.
Bibliography: p.
1. Trade-unions and foreign policy—Soviet Union.   2. Soviet
Union—National security.   3. International labor activities—
Political aspects—Europe.   4. Communist strategy.   5. Soviet
Union—Foreign relations—Europe.   6. Europe—Foreign
relations—Soviet Union.   I. Godson, Roy, 1942-   Kremlin
and labor.   II. Title.   III. Series: Strategy papers (National
Strategy Information Center); no. 40.
HD6490.F582S653   1984   331.88′0947
83-27116   ISBN 0-8448-1472-5 (pbk.)

Printed in the United States of America

Table of Contents

Foreword

Despite the ideological pretensions of the Soviet system to be a "workers' state," the aspirations of workers are consistently denied by a self-selected Communist Party elite that has often been described as a "new class." The brutal destruction of Poland's Solidarity union movement is only the latest in a long list of contradictions between the reality of Soviet policies and the illusions of communist propaganda. Even the irony of a George Orwell could scarcely encompass the obliteration of free trade unions by a power elite who base their empire on a moral appeal to strike off the chains of the proletariat.

Seldom has the Soviet Union been so visible in its contempt for the human rights of those citizens whose nations remain under its control as in Poland. Yet, for careful students of contemporary affairs, the crushing of a workers' movement by the managers of the "workers' state" comes as no surprise. Nor should it prove surprising that those same power brokers in Moscow would constantly seek to manipulate and exploit workers in the non-communist world to advance Soviet political and ideological dominance.

The variety of gambits by which they cynically try to subvert free trade unions in the West and Third World is the subject of this important study by a scholar intimately connected with the labor movement. Since the mid-1970s, Dr. Roy Godson has published and taught courses on the role of labor in world affairs. In 1977 he wrote a pioneering work on the role of labor in Soviet strategy, *The Kremlin and Labor,* for the National Strategy Information Center.

Since that time, events have shown that Soviet strategems for co-opting this crucial sector have continued, and in some cases have intensified. In this revised and updated version, Dr. Godson follows up on his earlier work with new data and analyses which bear out his contention that the West must achieve a greater awareness of Moscow's global political/labor offensive.

We are particularly pleased and honored to acknowledge the important contribution to this work by Irving Brown, Director of International Affairs of the AFL-CIO. I have known Irving for over thirty years, since the early Marshall Plan days when Stalinist operatives threatened to dominate the fledgling trade unions of war-torn Europe. Fortunately, owing to his heroic efforts and the efforts of the American labor movement, these communist designs were frustrated. Since 1945 he has been an international affairs specialist for the American labor movement, and for the past decade has served as the U.S. Worker-Delegate to the International Labor Organization (ILO). He is universally recognized as one of the world's leading experts on labor and world affairs, and his singular commitment to the promotion of free trade unions on four continents is legendary.

Frank R. Barnett
President
National Strategy Information Center

Preface

The February 1917 abdication of Nicholas II, Czar of Imperial Russia, was a victory for democratic forces in Russia. The subsequent establishment of a Constituent Assembly furthered an evolutionary process which promised to culminate in a truly democratic government and society. The dissolution of the Assembly in the fall of 1917, engineered by Lenin's Bolsheviks with armed force, stifled this progress and eventually led to the foundation of a totalitarian Soviet state.

A similar fate befell Russia's budding trade unions and labor leaders. In the expanding economy of pre-revolutionary Russia, trade unions were founded and began to develop openly. Although many leaders of opposition political parties were forced to operate semi-clandestinely or in exile, trade unionists were permitted to play a public role in the campaign for democratization of the czarist regime. Their participation with other political forces in the February revolution was critical to its success.

One must be impressed when reviewing the political activity of Russian workers, first through their trade unions, and later through the *Soviets* (Councils of Workers' and Soldiers' Deputies). Clearly the situation in Russia represented one of the earliest examples of active worker participation in a modern political struggle of a revolutionary nature. For it must be remembered that the major centers of political power and agitation were located in the cities, particularly Petrograd and

Moscow. The workers and peasants of the vast Russian countryside were largely uninvolved in the revolutionary activity of 1917, though they certainly participated in the Russian civil war which followed the Bolshevik seizure of power. The interests of the peasants were to be defended in the demands of the political parties, and expressed in Lenin's slogan, "Peace, Bread, Land." Their banners were carried by the political workers' organizations located in the cities.

The Bolsheviks, once in power, showed little gratitude for the decisive performance of the workers and their elected union leaders. After brutally crushing the Kronstadt uprising, Soviet leaders began a systematic elimination of trade unions as independent representative bodies.

Until 1927 there were constant factional struggles within the Bolshevik leadership on the nature and role of trade unions. Initially there were acute differences between those who favored truly independent trade unions (e.g., Rykov and Tomsky), and those who advocated the "militarization of labor," such as Trotsky, particularly after he became War Commissar. Within these extreme poles, Lenin, Stalin, and party theorist Bukharin assumed varying positions. Eventually, all nuances faded, and under Stalin the subjugation of all labor organizations to the Communist Party was total. "Trade unions" became, and remain today, mere transmission belts to fulfill the political directives of the Party and the State. Labor leaders are hand picked by Party bureaucrats, and their duties are to execute, not to initiate, orders and policies.

In recent years Soviet workers have grown increasingly restive. Deteriorating economic and social conditions have led to occasional strikes and sporadic attempts to form independent trade unions. One of the first figures to achieve notoriety in this connection was Vladimir Klebanov, a coal miner. According to several reports, Klebanov is now incarcerated in a psychiatric hospital, effectively eliminated from future activity.

At present, a free Soviet trade union organization, called SMOT, exists to some extent, but there is no evidence that it constitutes a significant force. Even so, valiant efforts are still underway to keep SMOT alive in the face of KGB harassment and persecution, including arrests, trials, and imprisonment of SMOT leaders.

By and large, worker unrest in the totalitarian Soviet system is manifested in more subtle forms. It appears in the low rates of productivity, increasing absenteeism, and chronic alcoholism. Soviet leaders, including Brezhnev and Andropov, have spoken about such problems afflicting Soviet society in open and frank terms. Andropov, in his declaratory exhortations to the Soviet labor force, went further than any previous Soviet leader in addressing these issues. Will the Soviet regime institute new disciplinary measures and enforcement of severe penalties on workers and their leaders, as has been the case in the past? Or, will the Kremlin initiate an overhaul of the Soviet "trade union" organization, permitting relatively more freedom for the unions in the hope of greater production? If the latter policy is adopted, the Politburo would have a potent response to the growing worldwide criticism of the Soviet system.

At present, of course, it is too early to assess the Soviet leadership's real intentions. There is growing sentiment in certain circles that the situation in Poland in the early 1980s, compounded by labor strife throughout the Soviet bloc, may affect the future status of labor not only in the U.S.S.R., but in other communist nations as well. Evidence of this trend is suggested by the ways in which Polish and Soviet government spokesmen have tried to insist that their labor legislation complies with International Labor Organization (ILO) conventions on freedom of association and collective bargaining. Soviet arguments on this issue have been repeatedly rejected by the ILO Governing Body. What is significant, however, is that Soviet leaders and their satellite regimes are not completely deaf to world public opinion, especially as expressed by trade unions in Europe, the United States, and the developing countries.

It may become important for the Soviets to continue in this direction if the free trade unions of the world persist in questioning the legitimacy of labor organizations in the Soviet Union and Eastern Europe. Since the Soviets apparently feel the need for a trade union instrument in foreign affairs, such as the World Federation of Trade Unions (WFTU), they eventually will be pressed to develop a more credible trade union structure within the U.S.S.R. itself.

Developments in this direction are by no means inevitable. Internal liberalization of Soviet policy will depend largely on the steadfastness of the free trade unions. If the artificial or cosmetic gestures of the Soviets in the labor sector are persistently rejected, then there may be hope for gradual change. The subjective forces of free trade unions and the objective forces of economic necessity may bear heavily on future decisions of the leaders of the communist nations.

Professor Roy Godson has provided us with a well-researched monograph on the fundamental nature of Soviet labor organizations and their role in Soviet foreign policy. The subject has all too often been ignored by Western scholars. This study is recommended as an introduction to the subject for trade unionists and scholars alike. The ability and competence of the author have been consistently demonstrated in his many books and articles, and now once again in this valuable addition to the literature on Soviet labor and foreign policy.

Irving Brown
Director
Department of International Affairs
AFL-CIO

Introduction

Few Western specialists have paid attention to the role of organized labor in Soviet strategy. While many agree that the Soviet leadership employs political tools in addition to military, economic, and cultural instruments, the role of organized labor has been ignored almost completely in discussions of Soviet objectives and methods, and in assessments of Soviet influence in the non-communist world.[1]

The primary purpose of this study is to demonstrate that organized labor is indeed a significant instrument of Soviet policy. While the importance of the subject and the objectives and tactics employed have varied over time, the behavior of the Soviet leadership particularly reveals its belief that labor can be a useful means for helping to shift the global power balance in its favor. Moscow is presently investing considerable human and material resources to influence the labor sector throughout the non-communist world, and some of these efforts already have begun to pay handsome dividends.

---

[1] A cursory examination of the index of any recent study of Soviet foreign policy leads to this conclusion. See, for example, Joseph Nogee and Robert Donaldson, *Soviet Foreign Policy Since World War II* (New York: Pergamon, 1981); Alvin Rubinstein, *Soviet Foreign Policy Since World War II: Imperial and Global* (Cambridge, Mass.: Winthrop, 1981); Kurt London, ed., *The Soviet Union in World Politics* (Boulder, Col.: Westview, 1980). Even U.S. government publications usually do not analyze labor; see, for example, the unclassified annual series on *Communist Aid to the Less Developed Countries*, which was terminated in the mid-1970s, or the USIA journal *Problems of Communism*.

The second purpose of the study is to draw policy implications from these conclusions. One which stands out clearly is that the Soviet use of organized labor, and the Western reaction to it, merit much closer study and attention. If we are to understand fully the importance of the subject and infer useful policy considerations, we need to know much more about the role of organized labor in domestic and international affairs, how the Soviets operate with labor groups, and how effective they can be. It would also be helpful to understand Western governmental and nongovernmental reaction to Soviet activities in the labor field. Outside of the AFL-CIO, however, the subject has been more or less ignored in the United States in recent years. Why do business, academic, and government circles believe Soviet efforts to gain control of the labor movement to be of little importance?

A comprehensive understanding of Soviet labor activities also would provide us with another indicator of the direction of overall Soviet behavior. Such an analysis can yield important data about Soviet objectives and methods on a global as well as a regional level. For example, in the 1970s Moscow made considerable efforts, both overtly and covertly, to bolster the strength of labor unions controlled by Western European communist parties. This campaign leads to the conclusion that, far from being completely unhappy with "Eurocommunism," Moscow was still trying to augment the influence of what it regarded as an important pro-Soviet force in Europe. Thus a study of Soviet labor activities is not only important for those concerned with nonmilitary instruments; it also has a more general application for students of overall Soviet strategy.[2]

---

[2]The international role of Soviet labor organizations may also tell us something about internal struggles in the Kremlin. In the 1920s, for example, Mikhail Tomsky, a member of the Politburo and Chairman of the All-Union Central Council of Trade Unions (AUCCTU), apparently attempted to use the AUCCTU's international contacts to increase the labor organization's independence from the Communist Party and enhance his ability to support the anti-Trotsky line in the Politburo. See Daniel F. Calhoun, *The United Front, The TUC and the Russians, 1923–28* (London: Cambridge University Press, 1976), especially pp. 22–23. Some 50 years later, another Chairman of the AUCCTU, and member of the Politburo, Aleksandr Shelepin, may have at-

Another major implication of this study is that there is a need for action. What those concerned with preventing the growth of Soviet influence in the non-communist world should do is beyond the purview of this study. But, as the data presented here suggest, the Soviets are seeking to weaken genuinely democratic trade unions and to reduce U.S. and Western power and influence throughout the world. Sometimes they have deliberately sought short-term gains, but generally the Soviets view the labor sector in long-range terms. Moreover, they may gain much more over the long run than they have during the past few years. In some regions, besides launching humanitarian programs to assist foreign workers, American nongovernmental organizations such as the AFL-CIO are doing a great deal to stem the spread of Soviet or Soviet-backed influence. But in other areas, there has been no American or Western presence to counteract or contain Soviet activities, and the consequences of this situation are unlikely to benefit the democratic labor movement or the West.

The present study is divided into two parts. The first section is concerned with Soviet perspectives on the role of labor in international affairs. How do the Soviets think about the use of organized labor? Soviet positions on certain aspects of this subject have shifted from time to time, usually as a reflection of broader changes in Soviet foreign policy perspectives. By and large, however, they were fairly consistent through the 1970s and early 1980s.

For the most part, information about these perspectives can be found in current Soviet sources. The writings of Soviet leaders and senior Party and labor analysts generally provide an accurate indicator of Soviet perspectives. On the other hand, Soviet views on the specific means by which labor in foreign countries can be used to enhance Soviet strategic objectives are not discussed publicly. Here it is necessary to study past Soviet

---

tempted to use international labor diplomacy to bolster his position and move the Soviet elite in his preferred direction. On possible differences between Shelepin and some of his Politburo colleagues, see, for example, Ilana Dimant, *Pravda and Trud, Divergent Attitudes Towards the Middle East*, Research Paper No. 3, Soviet and East European Research Center, Hebrew University, Jerusalem, 1972.

practice. For decades, the Soviet leadership has used organized labor to influence political and military conditions abroad, and almost never discussed the subject publicly. To some extent, specific usages must have become institutionalized in Soviet thinking. With the exception of previous policies which were judged seriously mistaken and thus abandoned, the historical record may be examined as a reasonable guide to current Soviet perspectives.

Some will assert that Soviet statements are mere rhetoric, and should not be taken seriously. This may be true, of course. Few students of strategy and foreign policy would take the statements of any single actor as the sole indicator of policy direction. But official statements do offer one indication that the leadership considers organized labor to be a significant force in world affairs.

Another indication can be found in Soviet practice. After discussing labor policy formulation and implementation, and the role of the Soviet-controlled World Federation of Trade Unions (WFTU), Moscow's efforts to use organized labor to help tip the world balance of power in its favor will be described and assessed. The data for this second section are drawn from a wide variety of Soviet and Western sources, including interviews conducted in the 1970s with current and former Soviet and WFTU officials and Western and non-Western union leaders.

It should be noted that in this study the term "Soviet," as opposed to "Russian," refers to the U.S.S.R., its policies, and its officials. The term "labor organizations" refers to workers' organizations controlled by ruling communist parties or other governmental elites. An effort will be made throughout to distinguish "labor organizations" from what in the West are referred to as "trade unions"—organizations designed to protect workers' interests which are not controlled by a governmental elite.[3]

---

[3]On the complexities of the distinction between trade unions and labor organizations, see William A. Douglas, *Trade Union Freedom and Human Rights, An Index Approach to Measurement*, Institute for Conflict and Policy Studies, Special Report Series, October 1977.

Finally, the author wishes to acknowledge the assistance of numerous scholars and practitioners of international affairs, as well as scores of trade union officials, in the preparation of the first edition of this study, *The Kremlin and Labor* (New York: Crane, Russak, 1977), as well as their assistance in this revised and updated volume. The author is particularly indebted to the research assistance and the skill, patience, and encouragement of members of the staff of Georgetown University's International Labor Program, and to William C. Bodie, Associate Editor at the National Strategy Information Center.

1

Soviet Perspectives on the Role of Labor in World Politics

The Significance of Labor

For the Soviet leadership, the "working class" and its institutions are the most important forces in history. They maintain that "working class" parties, labor organizations, and trade unions are crucially important in world politics. As these institutions are "strengthened" and "unified" under the leadership of communist parties throughout the world, ultimately the balance—or what the Soviets call the "correlation of forces" will tip decisively in favor of "socialism" and lead to the demise of the capitalist powers.

In the Soviet Union, the Communist Party of the Soviet Union (CPSU) is the most important working class institution. Because the "working class" is in power, the CPSU "represents" the interests of all the people in both domestic and foreign affairs. All other institutions must follow its "leadership." This is especially important for major social organizations such as the national "trade union" center, the All-Union Central Council of Trade Unions (AUCCTU).[1]

In fact, the labor organizations insist that they follow unswervingly the precise foreign policy directives of the Party. At the 16th Congress of the AUCCTU, for example, the "delegates declared their total support for the CPSU Central Committee's political course and activity, and assured it that trade union organizations would make every effort to implement the decisions of the 25th CPSU Congress."[2] In March 1982, at the 17th Congress of the AUCCTU, its new Chairman, Stepan Shalayev, described party leadership as the "source of the strength of the trade unions" which "pursue no objectives other than those set by the Communist Party."[3] Other examples of this unswerving support can be found in periodic AUCCTU Plenum statements:

> The AUCCTU Plenum assured the CPSU Central Committee that the Soviet trade unions will continue to make every effort to contribute, through their international activity, to the successful, practical implementation of the CPSU's foreign policy.[4]

> The Plenum unanimously approved the draft of the CPSU Central Committee for the 25th CPSU Central Committee Plenum and the conclusions and propositions contained in Brezhnev's speech.[5]

The March, 1982 Plenum approved a report on AUCCTU activity which in its very title makes clear the subordination of the unions to the party: "Account of the AUCCTU's Work and the Tasks of the U.S.S.R.'s Trade Unions in the Light of the 26th CPSU Congress' Decisions".[6]

---

[1]See, for example, T. S. Yampolskaya, *Social Organizations in the Soviet Union* (Moscow: Progress Publishers, 1975), p. 53. "The unions perform their tasks under the direct leadership of the CPSU and in close contact with the system of Soviets and the sectoral apparatus of the state administration."

[2]*Trud*, March 23, 1977.

[3]"Soviet Trade Union Congress Reaffirms Leninist Line", *Background Brief*, Foreign and Commonwealth Office, London, April 1982, p. 1.

[4]"An AUCCTU Plenum," *Trud*, May 23, 1975.

[5]Moscow Radio's Domestic Service, Foreign Broadcast Information Service (hereafter referred to as FBIS), December 30, 1975.

[6]FBIS, March 11, 1982, p. R-4., "Trud Carries AUCCTU Plenum-related Materials".

Outside the Soviet Union and other states ruled by communist parties (the "world socialist system"), the Soviet leadership sees the AUCCTU's main task—in addition to promoting Soviet foreign policy in general—as advancing and strengthening working class unity. This means, of course, unifying the working class under the leadership of its most "advanced elements," the communist parties, as well as undermining non-communist leaders who are alleged to be splitting the working class. The stress on working class unity under the leadership of the communist party is one of the most important points in Soviet doctrine. For example, an authoritative book edited by V. V. Zagladin, the first deputy head of the CPSU International Department, maintains that:

> The struggle for working class unity is one of the major tasks confronting the world Communist movement. In many respects, the prospects for peace, democracy, and socialism hinge on the accomplishment of that task. The unification of all workers in a single class force is a most important principle in the strategy and tactics of the world's Communists.[7]

Important promulgators of Soviet doctrine in this area, such as Zagladin (who was promoted in 1981 to a full member of the Central Committee) and other specialists on the international labor movement, frequently are fond of citing Lenin to make the same point:

> Unity is infinitely precious, and infinitely important to the working class. Disunited the workers are nothing. United they are everything.[8]

They also cite statements such as that of the 1969 meeting of Communist and Workers' Parties to demonstrate that the international communist movement recognizes this:

> The restoration of unity in the trade union movement, where it is split, as well as on the international scale, is essential for height-

[7]V. V. Zagladin, ed., *The World Communist Movement* (Moscow: Progress Publishers, 1973), p. 188.
[8]V. I. Lenin, *Collected Works*, vol. 19, p. 519.

ening the role of the working class in political life and the successful defense of its interests.[9]

In order to achieve unity, Soviet leaders believe they have to eradicate the divisions in the working class which lead some workers to follow communists, others to follow the social democrats and the "petty bourgeois and bourgeois parties," and still others to stand outside the political struggle altogether. What underlies this disunity? In the Soviet view, one must first consider the nature of the working class. It is derived from the heterogeneous racial, ethnic, religious, and economic composition of the work force. Secondly, for the Soviets, there are the activities of the "bourgeoisie." Fearing the power of a united working class, the "bourgeoisie" does everything in its power to "bribe" the workers and prevent the development of working class unity.

The struggle for unity among working class political parties, particularly socialist and communist parties, is one of the highest Soviet priorities. Speaking in 1978 to a meeting of social democratic parties, Boris Ponomarev, *de facto* head of the CPSU International Department, stated: "Our party advocated and advocates cooperation with the social democrats, above all, in questions of peace and detente," and invited a delegation of the Socialist International to visit Moscow.[10] At the 26th CPSU Congress in 1981 Chairman Brezhnev "spoke glowingly of the new and warm relationships between Socialist parties in several countries and the CPSU. Brezhnev also noted renewed contacts between leaders of the Socialist International and the CPSU, urging both movements to join hands in the interests of peace and the improvement of the international situation. Brezhnev noted that one major theme for Socialist-Communist cooperation should be disarmament."[11]

Along with this desired unity of leftist political parties, unity

[9]Zagladin, *op. cit.*, p. 229.

[10]L. Moskvin, *The Working Class and Its Allies* (Moscow: Progress Publishers, 1980), p. 274.

[11]Hans Janitschek, "The Contemporary Socialist International", in Ralph M. Goldman, ed., *Transnational Parties in World Affairs* (Lanham, Maryland:University Press of America, 1983).

within the labor movement is also of major significance. This significance, according to Soviet spokesmen, results from trade unions being the largest "mass" nonparty organization, with a membership embracing workers of the most varying views.[12] Their importance has increased along with their growing membership. Moscow maintains that by the late 1970s, 130 million people were members of trade unions, as opposed to 65 million in 1945 and 15 million in 1913. The effectiveness of the unions in the "anti-imperialist" struggle will increase, they believe, as more and more workers join unions and unity among workers with varying viewpoints is achieved. To become more effective, the trade unions—like other working class institutions—must increase their strength, overcome internal divisions, and rebuff the "splitting activities of the bourgeoisie."[13]

There are three major interrelated methods or principles through which working class institutions can be strengthened and unified, on national as well as on international levels. First, the workers must become deeply embroiled in the "revolutionary struggle." Unity cannot be imposed from the outside. By struggling together against the prevailing economic order and defending their interests, the workers will gradually understand the need for unification. To emphasize this point, Lenin is often quoted: "Unity must be won, and only the workers, the class-conscious workers themselves, can win it—by stubborn and persistent effort."[14]

Second, and related to the revolutionary struggle, there must be close cooperation between the unions and the workers' "most advanced representatives," the communist party. As Zagladin puts it: "Wherever Communist influence on the trade unions is stronger, the proletariat's class consciousness is greater, as is its militancy, and trade union participation in the political struggle is broader."[15] Cooperation with com-

[12]Zagladin *op. cit.* p. 220.
[13]Georgii Kanaev, *Soviet Trade Unions and the International Trade Union Movement* (Moscow: Novosti Press, 1970), pp. 6–7. Kanaev was deputy head of the AUCCTU's International Affairs Department.
[14]*Ibid.*, p. 3.
[15]Zagladin, *op. cit.*, p. 220.

munists prevents the trade unions from becoming "class collaborators" (who merely try to improve the lives of the workers in small ways), and reduces the effectiveness of the "splitting" tactics of the bourgeoisie.

The specific type of relations communists are to maintain with the unions, however, is not clearly stated in Soviet sources. On the one hand, the unions are to remain "independent." They are not to become "branches of the Party" lest this lead to the "isolation of the trade unions" and their "divorce from the masses." Experience has shown, Zagladin observes, that this will happen with the organization of "purely Communist trade unions." On the other hand, the extent to which communists are to control the unions is vague. Communists "are working for the closest possible contacts with the trade unions and are firmly opposed to any underestimation of communist activities in trade union ranks. Communists working in the trade unions are out to have the latter best accomplish the tasks confronting them."[16] Zagladin and others then go on to cite Lenin on these tasks.

Lenin, of course, argued against trade union "neutrality," that is, restricting the trade unions to economic concerns and having them remain neutral on political matters. Instead, the unions were to involve themselves in direct political activities. They were to serve as political schools for the working class and as a means for defending their political as well as economic interests. In these tasks, communists were to work closely with the unions and link them with the Party's "aims and ideals."[17]

The third principle to be used in strengthening and unifying the workers is "proletarian internationalism." Proletarian internationalism, a leading Soviet labor official has stated, "is a major ideological basis of the entire activity of Soviet trade

---

[16]*Ibid.*

[17]For Lenin's views about trade unions and politics, see *V. I. Lenin on Trade Unions, Collected Articles and Speeches* (Moscow: Progress Publishers, 1970); and Thomas Hammond, *Lenin on Trade Unions and Revolution* (New York: Columbia University Press, 1957).

unions."[18] This apparently means that working people throughout the world have common interests and help each other in the attainment of their common objectives. Soviet workers and their organizations recognize these interests and are struggling to assist workers and their organizations everywhere. As a result, proletarian internationalism has become "a powerful instrument in uniting the working class, all working people and revolutionary and democratic forces in various countries, in their struggle against the exploiting classes."[19]

A variety of specific tactics can be subsumed under the rubric of proletarian internationalism. Among the most significant are (a) defending the Soviet revolution and its significance as a worldwide social force; (b) material and fraternal assistance to working class forces throughout the world; and (c) dialogue on both the national and international levels with trade unions representing different points of view on the need for cooperation and unity.

With this general perspective in mind, the Soviet leadership maintains that, in general (that is, with some exceptions), the working class in capitalist countries is the most promising revolutionary force today. Soviet analysts state that this class comprises about 230 million people, and for the most part is located in North America, Western Europe, and Japan. It is, they insist, the most organized class and has acquired rich experience of the class struggle. The objective preconditions are ripe for a transition from capitalism to socialism in these countries; but the revolutionary process is developing slowly and unevenly, "since the revolutionary movement is confronted by a highly organized and experienced enemy."[20] One of the major long-term tasks of trade unions in these countries is to "curb the power of the monopolies." The unions are to do this by increasing their influence over all phases of economic and political life, especially by demands for nationalization and control of key industries. If the unions and other working class

---

[18]K. A. Guseinov, *Trade Union Association: U.S.S.R., Asia and Africa* (Moscow: Nauka Publishers, 1967), p. 5.

[19]Zagladin, *op. cit.*, p. 441.

[20]*Ibid.*, p. 94.

institutions acquire control of the economy, they will be in a strong position to unify the workers.

From the late 1920s up until approximately the death of Stalin, the Kremlin—in its doctrine, at least—made little distinction between the Third World and the capitalist countries. With the 20th Party Congress in 1956, Moscow acknowledged that all states were not necessarily members of either the Socialist or the capitalist camp. There were "in-between" states in the Third World, and they presented the Soviet Union with new and different problems, as well as important opportunities. Specifically, their nationalism and reaction to Western colonial rule made them natural allies for the major anti-imperialist powers—the Soviet Union and its allies. Indeed, in Soviet judgment the "national liberation forces" in the Third World became not only "one of the main elements of the world anti-imperialist movement," but allies of the communist states and non-bloc communist parties in a joint offensive against imperialism and capitalism as a system of social relations.[21]

For the non-Western peoples, this movement involved, in the first stage, liberation from colonial rule, and in the second stage, establishing genuine independence from neocolonial hegemony and the national bourgeoisie. The second stage of the national liberation struggle and the governments it has produced has received various Soviet designations—national democracy and revolutionary democracy—to define stages somewhere between capitalism and a socialist state.

Nevertheless, Moscow insists that until a communist party has obtained a monopoly of power or a "revolutionary party" becomes Marxist-Leninist in theory and in practice, these regimes do help create favorable conditions for the advent of "socialism." They are not in themselves "socialist." The Soviet leaders still assert that the working class and its vanguard must be in power if there is to be a completely satisfactory political change. Indeed, they frequently classify a regime primarily

[21]Leon Gouré and Morris Rothenberg, *Soviet Penetration of Latin America* (Miami, Fla.: Center for Advanced International Studies, 1975), p. 10. The entire first chapter of this monograph is devoted to changing Soviet perspectives on the Third World and particularly Latin America.

according to the role of the communist party and other working class institutions. Moscow recognizes a variety of possibilities. They can range from communist participation in government with other "democratic forces"—including those of a bourgeois character to which, for the moment, they have to concede leadership—to ideological purity in opposition. The key tactic is increasing the strength and unity of working class forces under the leadership of vanguard cadres.

Current Opportunities

As the Soviets see the Third World now, there is a distinction between most of Africa, the Middle East, and Asia, on the one hand, and Latin America on the other. These areas have a number of distinct historic, economic, and political characteristics, and as a result present different opportunities for the Soviets.

For Moscow, the newly independent states of Africa and Asia, which only recently threw off the colonial yoke, now have an opportunity to develop along a "non-capitalist" path. They are not bound to develop along the lines of the capitalist states, nor even along lines of Latin America, which the Soviets see as basically capitalist. Instead, they can reduce the power of "international monopolies" and the private sector, and increase the influence of the Socialist camp and the state sector until they are ready for the transition to communism.

The Afro-Asian states, the Soviets maintain, are still suffering from the legacy of colonialism. During the many centuries of European rule, exploitation of the population was based on a divide-and-rule principle. Deliberately and systematically, the "colonialists fostered strife amongst the enslaved nations and tribes, and then acted as pacifiers saving them from mutual destruction."[22] The economies of these areas were converted into colonial appendages, supplying the West with raw materials. The result was economic stagnation, little industry, and a very small, weak, and poorly organized proletariat.

[22]Guseinov, *op. cit.*, p. 8.

These circumstances led the incipient trade union movement to develop in specific directions. First, according to Soviet analysts, Asian and African unions were neutral in political terms. They engaged in economic, as opposed to political, activities because their roots were in reformist Western unions. Second, they were "isolated" on the national as well as the continental scale. The same "monopoly capital" prevented them from unifying in the past, and still prevents the unification of these forces today. "Progressive forces" within various labor movements are victimized and purged, and attempts are made to prevent union leaders from learning about the Soviet model and bringing about the unification of workers on a continental basis.

In the 1970s and 1980s, the Soviets maintain, the main struggle of these countries is along the "non-capitalist path" of development. They have to build an anti-imperialist national democratic front of progressive forces. The precise composition of the front may be different in different countries and stages, but the working class, although small, will be the most revolutionary group in the long run. In the first stage of the liberation struggle, the overthrow of colonialism, the workers' class interests coincided in the main with the interests and struggle of the entire nation. Since then, the national bourgeoisie has begun to defend its interests to the detriment of the rest of the country. Hence, the working class now has to struggle against the remnants of imperialism from abroad and the local bourgeoisie at home. The trade unions have to be bolstered and unified on both the national and international planes as part of this effort.

For the Soviets, Latin America has special characteristics. First, it is a more advanced region. As a result of having achieved independence in the 19th century, Latin American countries embarked on the capitalist road to development many years ago. But this type of capitalist system was retarded by its dependence on the large industrial countries, particularly the United States, which provided it with technology and investments. In turn the industrial nations became the principal markets of the region.

Soviet analysts also maintain that there is great unevenness in the economic and political development of the region. They point to different political conditions and alignments in various countries, giving rise to different revolutionary opportunities. Politically and ideologically, Latin American regimes range through the entire spectrum of Soviet typology—from reactionary pro-imperialist governments (for example, Paraguay and Brazil) in the 1970s, to nationalist-reformist bourgeois regimes (Colombia and Venezuela in the same decade) to "progressive," "democratic," or even "revolutionary democratic" systems, as in Chile under Allende or represented in varying degrees by the military governments of Peru, Panama, and Ecuador in the 1970s.

The "contradictions" or results of these special types of societies are also somewhat different from those at work in Africa and Asia. First, there is a powerful nationalist mass movement in the continent which assumes a more or less pronounced anti-imperialist, anti-capitalist character, unlike nationalist movements in many other Third World areas. The movement consists of the merged results of the contradictions between (a) the peasants and semifeudal landlords; (b) the urban proletariat and a rather highly developed bourgeoisie; and (c) the national aspirations of the people and the interests of the foreign exploiters. Second, according to Boris Ponomarev, the CPSU Secretary with responsibility for the nonruling international communist movement, a strong working class has developed in Latin America "with considerable experience in revolutionary struggle." "All Latin American countries have communist parties, and in many countries they are big and influential." The social democratic movement, however, "does not have profound roots in the labor movement on the continent and does not enjoy a major influence."[23]

In the 1960s Moscow recognized that the relative weakness of the Latin American communist parties made it unlikely that they could attain power by themselves or through violent rev-

[23]"Topical Problems in the Theory of the World Revolutionary Process," *Kommunist* (Moscow), October 1971.

olution. Instead, they were encouraged to seek a "peaceful transition to socialism" by taking advantage of the more advanced industrial economies and the better organized labor movements in Latin America, and by forging new alliances with other "revolutionary anti-imperialist and democratic forces." "These involve the working class, peasantry, the petty and middle bourgeoisie, the patriotic military, and even such sections of the bougeoisie which, under certain conditions, find themselves involved in contradiction with monopoly capitalism and are objectively interested in opposing imperialist penetration."[24]

The strategy of the "peaceful transition to socialism," in addition to promoting such broad class alliances, also had two other features. First, it required rejection of the Castroite guerilla forces in Latin America, whose calls for immediate and violent rebellion would frighten away potential communist allies in the "patriotic military" and the "petty and middle bourgeoisie." Second, this strategy placed primary Soviet emphasis on state-to-state relations with existing governments in Latin America, rather than on particularly economic relations, supporting guerilla movements to topple those governments.

Soviet enthusiasm for the "peaceful transition" peaked with the victory of Allende's Popular Unity coalition in the Chilean elections of 1970. The Soviet "peaceful transition" strategy appeared to be successful. Within three years, however, General Pinochet's coup overthrew the Allende government, more conservative generals replaced the neutralist Velasco regime in Peru, and the leftist United Front in Uruguay was defeated in elections and subsequently liquidated by a military coup.

Consistent with its new emphasis on global armed struggle, the Soviets in the late 1970s reversed their strategy in most of Latin America. The new approach advocated armed struggle, the integration of local communist parties and radical guerilla groups into joint politico-military fronts, and the overthrow of bourgeois governments from within rather than wooing

[24]Zagladin, *op. cit.*, p. 340.

them on a government-to-government basis from without.[25] The victory of the Sandinista politico-military front in Nicaragua in 1979 confirmed the Soviet enthusiasm for armed struggle, a policy which has continued into the early 1980s. Mainly in Latin America's more stable nations, such as Mexico and Venezuela, did the Soviets continue their 1960s emphasis on peaceful tactics, broad class alliances, and state-to-state relations.

Soviet Global Labor Strategy

Apart from working class forces in separate regions, the Soviets also believe that the international labor movement itself can play a role in shifting the balance of power further in their favor. They believe that unity among the global internationals (the World Federation of Trade Unions, the International Confederation of Free Trade Unions, and the World Confederation of Labor), regional labor organizations (the International Confederation of Arab Trade Unions, the Organization of African Trade Union Unity, the European Trade Union Confederation, and the Latin American regional labor bodies), as well as industrial internationals (see the Appendix) can play a role in weakening the West and furthering "world revolution." As a Soviet international labor specialist put it:

> Soviet leaders believe that unity of trade union action on a national, regional, and international scale will help to undermine the political and economic power of the monopolies. . . . Soviet trade unions believe that the tendency toward unity of different units (holding different political views) of the international trade union movement is an objective factor directly connected with the class interests of the working people and their vital needs. This tendency, despite all the machinations of the splitters of the proletariat, has always been the basis of the international trade union movement.[26]

---

[25]For a survey of the Soviet switch in strategies, see Robert S. Leiken, *Soviet Strategy in Latin America*, The Washington Papers, No. 93, (New York: Praeger, 1982), Chapters 3 and 4.

[26]Kanaev, *op. cit.*, pp. 55–56.

Soviet leaders see unprecedented opportunities to achieve their objectives in the present world situation. They maintain that the socialist world is gaining strength, while the capitalist world becomes increasingly unable to solve its problems; and thus the working people in both capitalist and Third World areas will come to realize the need for unity and a transition to socialism. As Ponomarev put it, the two most important processes during the 1970s were:

> . . . the growing might of countries of the Socialist community, their vigorous action together with all the peace forces against imperialist aggression, for detente and international security; and second, the mounting struggle of the working class and working people generally in the capitalist countries, of the ex-colonial peoples and anti-imperialist movement as a whole. Developing in interconnection, these two cardinal social processes have substantially changed the international situation in favor of peace and socialism.[27]

The Soviets maintain that in addition to their increased military strength, they and the Eastern European states have entered a new and higher phase of economic and political development. They also maintain that the achievements of "existing socialism made possible the historical change from the Cold War to detente and the consolidation of the principles of the peaceful coexistence of states with differing social systems."[28]

But "peaceful coexistence" for the Kremlin remains, as it has more or less since the time of Lenin, a strategy or stage that can be used to bring about the destruction of capitalism. As both Lenin and Stalin pointed out, states with different social systems can coexist for limited periods of time, and peaceful coexistence should be used to strengthen the communist camp. The major difference in peaceful coexistence now as compared with earlier periods, Soviet writers argue, is that there has been

---

[27]Boris Ponomarev, "The World Situation and the Revolutionary Process," *World Marxist Review*, June 1974, p. 3.
[28]*Ibid.*, p. 4.

a shift in Western thinking and policy.[29] While the Soviet Union has always been willing to follow the policy of peaceful coexistence, only in the 1970s did the West develop a more "sober" and "realistic" attitude. This shift in Western policy was caused, so this analysis goes, by the increasing crisis in the imperialist camp and the shifting power balance in favor of the Soviet Union. These factors caused the West to be more cautious in its dealings with the Soviet Union, and also forced the United States to establish closer economic relations with the Soviet Union in order to compete more effectively with rival capitalist states.

Although the degree of enthusiasm for detente varies somewhat among Soviet analysts, they generally agree that it will further the interests of the Soviet Union and only temporarily aid capitalism. In the long run, the contradictions of the imperialist camp will be heightened. Because the Soviet Union will no longer appear to be threatening, for example, it will become increasingly difficult for the Western military-industrial complex to justify its rule and maintain the cohesion of its military alliances. In the meantime, the power of the communist camp will grow, and there will be a gradual change in the "objective realities" of power in favor of the Soviet Union.

For Moscow, then, peaceful coexistence is a form of class struggle and a method of weakening the capitalist states. Even the use of force is not completely ruled out against capitalist countries, or even within the socialist camp. Although Stalin's successors have allowed the possibility that nuclear war between the two systems may not be fatalistically "inevitable," and that states representing different social systems can coexist without recourse to general violence, communists in the West have been warned that violence may be necessary in support of, or to protect, the revolution.

Apart from using detente to strengthen the Socialist camp economically, by obtaining credits, technology, and the like,

---

[29]For descriptions and analysis of Soviet views see R. Judson Mitchell, *Ideology of a Superpower* (Stanford, Cal.: Hoover Institution Press, 1982); John Lenczowski, *Soviet Perceptions of U.S. Foreign Policy* (Ithaca: Cornell University Press, 1982).

the ideological struggle is to be "intensified." This is not a trivial matter. It is not to be left exclusively to the propagandists. Political and economic struggle in general is to be increased. There is to be peaceful coexistence between states, but not between social classes. After the U.S.S.R. assisted with the intervention of Cuban military units in the Angolan civil war, Brezhnev explained: "Detente does not in the slightest abolish, and cannot abolish or alter, the laws of the class struggle. . . ."[30] The Soviet Union is to guard itself against Western efforts to take advantage of detente; and at the same time, the Soviet camp is to wage offensive ideological warfare.

The second major "phenomenon of our time," as the Soviets call it, the general crisis of capitalism, has entered into a distinctive third phase. (The first phase was the period following the Bolshevik Revolution and the establishment of the world communist movement, while the second took place in the 1930s and was highlighted by World War II). As Timour Timofeiev, Director of the U.S.S.R. Academy of Sciences Institute of the International Workers Movement, observes, the third phase is:

> . . . the crisis in the economic base of contemporary capitalism and the breakdown of the existing structure of the world's capitalist economic system, paralleled by a number of political, national, racial, and moral crises and drastic aggravation of social tension in the capitalist system as a whole. In other words, the intensifying general crisis of capitalism has become truly all-embracing.[31]

According to Boris Ponomarev:

> Never before have crisis processes in the economy, and the factors that deepen the political crisis in individual imperialist countries and in the whole system of capitalist international relations, been so closely interrelated, and never before have they so powerfully affected each other.[32]

[30]Foreign Policy Association, *Great Decisions '81*, New York, 1981, p. 9.
[31]Timour Timofeiev, "The Banner of the Revolutionary Struggle of the Proletariat; On Trends in the Class Struggle Under the Conditions of the Aggravation of the General Crisis of Capitalism," *Kommunist*, April 1975.
[32]Ponomarev, *loc. cit.*, p. 8.

The "crisis," the Soviets maintain, is manifest and can be seen in different areas—the energy crisis, the economic policy crisis, the overproduction crisis, and the political-ideological crisis. It also can be seen in (a) relations within individual capitalist countries, which are said to be characterized by unemployment, together with rapid inflation and production stagnation (stagflation); (b) relations between the capitalist countries, such as U.S. efforts to "exploit" its lead in oil and gas and "avenge" itself on the world market (symbolized by the collapse of the monetary system built on dollar supremacy), and the "counter-offensive" and "economic rivalry" of Western Europe and Japan; and (c) relations between the imperialist states and the Third World characterized by the "demands of the international monopolies for cheap raw materials and the response of the developing countries, which are asserting their sovereign right to dispose of the national wealth as they see fit."

This "crisis" also offers the communists unprecedented opportunities to help shift the world balance of forces. As Timofeiev stated in the theoretical organ of the CPSU, communists must observe:

> . . .the pulsebeat of all political life and the state of the organized labor movement and the feelings of the broadest possible toiling masses. It is precisely on the basis of such an analysis that the Communists are drawing the conclusion as to their real possibility to implement an aggressive strategy in the class struggle in a number of links within the world's imperialist system.[33]

Timofeiev then goes on to describe the most important characteristics of the third phase of the capitalist crisis. First is the expansion of the scale of strikes in many capitalist countries. His figures indicate that in 1965 there were 36 million strikers in the entire capitalist world (19 million in the advanced capitalist countries). By 1974, the figures had risen to 65 million strikers, and 47 million in advanced capitalist countries.

Second, the labor movement, to judge from its qualitatively

---

[33]Timofeiev, *loc. cit.*

24 *Roy Godson*

new level of demands, has become increasingly aggressive. Apart from defending their daily interests, the workers are opposing "ever more frequently and adamantly the foundations of the economic and socio-political course of the ruling circles." Then there is the increasing internationalization of the class struggle. Working people are launching joint action not only within national frameworks but on an international scale as well. Among the most significant of these are (a) international coordination against multinational corporations; (b) the "strengthening of international solidarity" with Third World countries which wish to dispose of their wealth as they see fit; and (c) the "solution" to the complex problems of the migrant workers, and the incorporation and unification of the 12 to 20 million migrant workers in Europe into the struggle of the entire proletariat.

Last, the processes contributing to the unification of a "broad front of popular forces" are developing quite rapidly. In the long run, these forces are related to the "scientific and technical revolution, and to the changes it has triggered in the social structure of society and the social structure of the working class, including the intensifying rapprochement between hired intellectuals and manual labor."[34]

These changes in the capitalist social structure have been intensified by the economic crisis; and the results are especially apparent in France and Italy, where alliances between communist and non-communist groups are being forged in both political and trade union circles. This is part of a two-stage revolution—democratic first and Socialist later. It also can be seen in Portugal and Peru, where the "proletarian vanguard" was able to make alliances with the military. In fact, Timofeiev states explicitly:

> The progressive organizations, including the Communists, see in the solid alliance with progressive military personnel a prerequisite for the further development of the anti-Fascist and general democratic struggle, and the timely implementation of the changes that have ripened in society.

[34]*Ibid.*

And he concludes his analysis of the resulting trends of the crisis:

> The developments in the 1970s in various parts of the capitalist world confirm the ripening of objective and subjective prerequisites needed for such a (revolutionary) change. The aggressive line of the Communist movement now stems from the need and increased real possibilities for an upsurge in the class struggle on a higher level.[35]

In 1982, the Tenth WFTU World Congress devoted the entire first section of the basic document it adopted to "The Deep Crisis of the Capitalist World," noting that the crisis had continued for almost a decade. As another WFTU document noted: "caught in a deep and lasting crisis of their system, monopoly capital seeks to find a way out through militarism and war, suppression of human rights and democratic liberties."[36]

In sum, the Soviets see the labor movement unified under communist party leadership as a highly useful means of weakening Western states and governments. Furthermore, their prospects for success have been enhanced by recent developments, such as the increased strength of the communist camp, the consolidation of the principles of peaceful coexistence (detente), and the current or third stage of the general crisis of capitalism. In general, labor in the advanced capitalist states is more susceptible to this type of activity than in other regions; but the Soviets also seem to believe there are many opportunities in the Third World for the labor movement to be developed and unified under communist leadership.

Specific Political-Military Usages

Yet the mechanisms by which the unified labor movement is to help shift the balance of forces in the direction of "socialism" have not been publicly specified by contemporary Soviet theoreticians. Nor have they discussed how labor can be used

[35]*Ibid.*
[36]*Trade Unions and the Challenges of the 1980s*, Main Document adopted by the 10th World Trade Union Congress, WFTU, Havana, 1982, p. 8; "General Declaration," in *Appeal and Resolutions*, 10th World Trade Union Congress, WFTU, Havana, 1982, p. 15.

as an instrument of policy—except, of course, as part of the Soviet effort to promote "world revolution." Once again, past practice provides significant clues to Soviet thinking. Unless there has been a radical break with past practice, there are at least six specific usages of organized labor which can be considered part of the Soviet perspective.

First, ever since the time of Lenin, communists have referred to trade unions as "schools of communism." That is to say, trade unions may be used to affect the political attitudes of workers. After all, the unions are a significant part of a mass movement, and they have enormous potential. They have access to millions of workers on a daily basis; on docks, ships, planes, and loading platforms, in factories, schools, and offices throughout the world. They can explain the root causes of the bad times and the good times; they can identify the workers' "enemies" and point to the workers' "friends." When well managed, the organizational talent, muscle, and financial resources of the trade unions can be a potent propaganda tool, capable of guiding workers' attitudes and affecting their behavior in activities ranging from street demonstrations to elections.

Second, they know that trade unions, on occasion, can be used to infiltrate the government of a modern industrial state. Most advanced industrial societies have found it useful to include former union leaders in governmental bodies, and many high-ranking union officials serve on government, industrial, and economic commissions as nominees of their own movement. Communist parties have been successful in placing former communist trade union officials in senior and junior posts, particularly when they have been part of a governing coalition. This was a successful tactic in the nationalized industries of France and Italy following World War II.[37]

The use of political as opposed to economic strikes is a third weapon the Soviet Union and communist parties have available. Economic strikes can be defined as those called to improve the wages and working conditions of union members, simply and directly, although such strikes often have inciden-

---

[37]Mario Einaudi, Maurice Bye, and Ernesto Rossi, *Nationalization in France and Italy* (Ithaca: Cornell University Press, 1951).

tal political effects. For example, strikes which succeed in maintaining the labor force's real purchasing power during an inflationary period can sustain strong consumer demand and prevent recession, thus supporting a government's popular standing. Conversely, economic strikes resulting in wage increases well beyond corporations' ability to pay may create an inflationary spiral which would undermine the incumbent government's position. Economic strikes, however, are not called to create such political repercussions. They are unintended side effects, and unions generally will try to hold political fallout to a minimum in these circumstances.

A political strike, on the other hand, is not called to improve the immediate economic lot of the workers, but rather to produce desired political consequences—instability, government reforms, or the removal of uncooperative officials. Improving the economic conditions of union members, if such should result from the political strike, is strictly incidental. Both democratic and non-democratic labor movements use political strikes. Democratic labor participated in general strikes seeking the resignation of General Somoza in Nicaragua in 1978, and Polish workers used a wave of strikes in 1980 to build their free union federation, *Solidarnosc*. Communist unions used political strikes in their efforts to sieze power in Portugal after the fall of the Salazar-Caetano dictatorship in 1974.

The Soviets are contemptuous of strikes which serve "merely" to improve the lot of the workers and are not part of an overall political strategy. These are considered pure "economism"—reformist activities which temporarily ameliorate the conditions of the workers, but which in fact are part of bourgeois efforts to split the working class. In Allende's Chile, for example, strikers were criticized because they were "infected by ideas of economism (which) caused considerable harm to the Chilean revolution and served as one of the factors which weakened the popular unity government."[38]

Perhaps the most significant use of political strikes to pro-

---

[38]A. I. Sobolev, "Questions of Strategy and Tactics of the Class Struggle at the Present Stage of the General Crisis of Capitalism," *Rabochiy Klass I Sovremenny Mir*, FBIS, February 19, 1975, p. A2.

mote Soviet objectives came in the immediate post-World War II period. During the late 1940s, Moscow ordered the European communist parties to use political strikes to impede economic recovery, wreck the Marshall Plan, and undermine NATO and Western defense efforts. Both before and after that period, the communists used political strikes in Europe and the Third World.[39]

In addition to using organized labor to support candidates, causes, and political strikes, the Soviets for many years have used labor for a variety of paramilitary activities. Obviously, information on these activities is very difficult to obtain. One of the most interesting confirmations of Soviet concern with the paramilitary uses of labor can be found in the writing of a former German communist, Richard Krebs, who settled in the United States in 1940 after 20 years as a communist organizer. In 1941 Krebs, under the pseudonym of Jan Valtin, published a sensational and flamboyant autobiography, *Out of the Night,* which became a best seller.[40] Krebs described his worldwide travels as a paid communist organizer, his capture and torture by the Gestapo, and finally his escape from both the Gestapo and the Soviet secret police. Two thirds of the book, however, is devoted to describing Krebs' training and his organizing of trade unions for purposes of espionage, staging *coups d'etat,* and creating paramilitary organizations to serve Russian ends.[41]

Soviet labor activities in Czechoslovakia in 1948 are an example of a *coup d'etat* strategy that they may also have tried to implement in other countries, such as postwar France and Italy. Their main approach was to get control of labor in strategic industries—transportation, communications, electricity, and printing. Political strikes were then called either to bring down the government or to demonstrate the unfeasability of

---

[39]For a description of communist political strikes against the Marshall Plan and NATO, see Roy Godson, *American Labor and European Politics, The AFL as a Transnational Force* (New York: Crane, Russak, 1976).

[40]Jan Valtin, *Out of the Night* (New York: Alliance, 1941).

[41]The U.S. government also released a number of declassified or sanitized intelligence reports on Soviet efforts in this regard in the early postwar period. Some are reprinted in their entirety in Godson, *op. cit.,* Appendix C.

effective government without communist participation. The communists then insisted on control of strategic ministries, preferably the police and the armed forces. While communist demands were not met completely, they could insist at least that determined anti-communists not control these sectors. Then, when it was judged propitious to seize actual power, the communists used their control of labor organizations to take over key sectors, or at least to impede the government's ability to maintain itself. In some circumstances, actions such as denying the government access to printing presses or the electronic media to mobilize people, or barring transportation for the armed forces could have proved decisive.[42] Similarly, the trade unions could be very important in consolidating and maintaining power in the aftermath of a coup. The Bolsheviks did just that, and labor "fronts" modeled on this pattern have been established in almost all areas which Moscow-oriented communists now control.[43]

The use of unions for espionage is also well known to the Kremlin. Apart from industrial espionage, unions can sometimes place workers in sensitive defense industries and installations. In postwar France, for example, communist union officials in the CGT were convicted of spying on military activities in the docks. Ultimately, the French government had to cease employing CGT-"approved" workers in the maritime industry, and take security precautions at defense-related institutions in other parts of the country.[44]

Finally, the Soviets are well aware that trade unions have a variety of other paramilitary uses. During World War II, for example, the Allied governments utilized the unions for

[42]On the attempted application of this tactic in France in 1947, see *ibid.*

[43]Jay B. Sorenson, *The Life and Death of Soviet Trade Unions, 1917–1928* (New York: Atherton, 1967). For an account of how free trade unions threatened the Bolsheviks after the October Revolution, as well as Lenin's views on the need for secret police control of the unions, see George Leggett, *The Cheka* (New York:Oxford University Press, 1981). See also AFL Free Trade Union Committee, *What Happened to Trade Unions Behind the Iron Curtain* (1947); Paul Barton, *Conventions Collectives Et Réalitiés Ouvrières En Europe De L'Est* (Paris: Editions Ouvrières, 1957); Force Ouvrière, *Les Ouvrières Face A La Dictature, 1938–1968* (Paris: Confédération Force Ouvrière, 1969).

[44]Godson, *op. cit.*

espionage, and also sabotage activities, in Nazi-occupied Europe.[45] After the war, the Soviets used communist-controlled unions first in propaganda activities against rearmament, and later to sabotage Western defense efforts.[46] They also planned to use communist-controlled trade unions as part of their underground apparatus either in the event communist parties were banned or if there was a war between the Soviet Union and the West. The postwar paramilitary use of labor was first reported by Western trade unionists who tried to neutralize these activities; and more recently, declassified CIA documents have helped to confirm these reports.[47]

Thus, organized labor has long been viewed by the Soviet leadership as a significant instrument of policy. The specific usages, of course, depended on their momentary objectives and expectations about what could be accomplished. Unless Soviet labor policy is merely declaratory or the Soviets have concluded that their past activities have been mistaken, misdirected, or simply ineffective today, these perspectives should provide a reasonable guide to future attempts to use labor throughout the world.

[45]Very little has been written about this, and it is impossible to obtain access to OSS Labor Division files. For a brief discussion of the OSS Labor Division, see *ibid.*, especially Appendix A. For a description of communist labor activities in the Resistance, see the communist CGT leader Andre Tollet's *La Classe Ouvrière Dans la Résistance* (Paris: Editions Sociales, 1969).

[46]William Douglas, "West German Communism As an Aid to Moscow," *World Affairs*, March 1970; and Godson, *op. cit.*

[47]See Godson, *op. cit.*, especially Appendix C.

2

Labor as an Instrument of Soviet Policy

Policy Formulation and Implementation

The Politburo of the CPSU is the key policymaking body of the Soviet Union. It determines Soviet objectives and orchestrates the instruments of policy. Tracing the formulation and implementation of Politburo policy with respect to organized labor, however, is problematic. From time to time, the Kremlin releases information on foreign-oriented labor activities, but several institutions which deal with labor matters are rarely discussed publicly. For example, the activities of Soviet intelligence agencies, which have been concerned with organized labor since the Bolshevik seizure of power, are seldom exposed to public gaze—at least deliberately. Almost certainly, however, the Politburo coordinates KGB programs with AUCCTU activities. Similarly, the Central Committee Secretariat, the Ministry of Foreign Affairs, the various research institutes, and possibly the GRU (Soviet military intelligence) are also involved in developing and executing Politburo decisions.[1]

[1]Presumably, the GRU is responsible for intelligence about Western military bases and defense production and transportation. This information can be obtained from military personnel who may be unionized, but also, as was discussed earlier, from civilians and union officials working on the bases or employed in military production and transportation.

There are indications that several key officials have major responsibilities for policymaking with respect to labor. Certainly during the 1970s one was Mikhail Suslov, who before his death in 1982 was one of the three senior Party Secretaries, and the man who usually chaired the weekly Politburo meetings in Brezhnev's absence. He had overall responsibilities for ideology, and for relations with ruling and nonruling Communist Parties and other institutions of the working class. Andrei Kirilenko, another senior Party Secretary and senior Politburo member, was responsible for overall coordination of Politburo and Party affairs. A third leading figure is Boris Ponomarev. As noted earlier, Ponomarev is a candidate member of the Politburo, one of ten CPSU Secretaries, and de facto head of the Central Committee's International Department. As the Politburo did not have its own staff, apart from Brezhnev's personal assistants, it is likely that this department, like other Central Committee departments, was accountable to the Politburo on these matters.

There are well over 100 professionals in the International Department. Subdivided into "sections," the Department deals with: nonruling communist parties, socialist-oriented parties and other parties which maintain relations with communist parties, as well as nongovernmental organizations. The Department, in turn, also appears to be serviced by a number of research centers belonging to the Social Sciences Section of the Presidium of the U.S.S.R. Academy of Sciences, such as the well known Institute of World Economics and International Relations (IMEMO), the Institute for the Study of the U.S.A. and Canada (IUSAC), and the lesser known Institute of the International Workers Movement (IMRD). There are also institutes dealing with Africa, Latin America, and the Far East.[2]

Some of the work of these institutes has been coordinated within the context of so-called Scientific Councils of Complex

[2]For a discussion of the role of foreign policy analysts in Soviet decisionmaking, see Oded Eran, *The "Mezhdunarodniki," Soviet Foreign Experts* (forthcoming); and Richard S. Soll, Arthur A. Zuelke, Jr., and Richard B. Foster, *The Role of Social Science Research Institutes in the Formulation and Execution of Soviet Foreign Policy*, Stanford Research Institute, Strategic Studies Center, March 1976, especially pp. 13–40.

Problems in order to avoid overlapping subject matter, and to yield a multidisciplinary output on a given problem. In 1961, for example, a Scientific Council on the Complex Problems of Economic Competition of the Two Systems was established; and a few years later, a Council on the Complex Problems of Working Class and Democratic Mass Movements in Capitalist Countries was created. Together, they began publication of an irregular "annual" serial, *Competition of the Two Systems*. The editorial board of this journal consisted of A. M. Rumyantsev (a member of the Central Committee), D. M. Gvishiani (Deputy Chairman of the State Committee for Science and Technology), G. A. Arbatov (Director of IUSAC), and N. N. Inosemtsev (Director of IMEMO), both candidate members of the Central Committee, the Directors of the Institutes of Far East and Africa Studies, and Timour Timofeiev, Director of the Institute of the International Workers Movement (IMRD).

The IMRD focuses almost exclusively on labor, and particularly international labor affairs. Unlike IUSAC, IMEMO, and the other institutes mentioned above, which are placed in the Economics Department of the Social Science Division, the IMRD—until the late 1970s, at least—was independently attached to the Social Science Division. Timofeiev, son of the American Communists Eugene and Peggy Dennis, reportedly was on good personal terms with Suslov and Ponomarev in the 1970s. The departments of the Institute conduct research in specific problem areas, such as complex theoretical problems of the "world revolutionary process;" the workers movement in the developed capitalist countries; social and economic positions of the workers; international organizations; trade union movements; and contemporary history and international problems of the workers movement.[3] Very few publications of this high-ranking and well-placed institute have been reviewed by Western scholars, and little is known in the United States about its work.

During the 1970s, there were several key officials active in

---

[3]O. N. Melikyan, "The Activity of the Institute of the International Workers Movement of the Academy of Sciences of the U.S.S.R.: Structure, Basic Directions of Research Works," *Competition of the Two Systems* (Moscow: Nauka, 1970), pp. 452–457.

the international labor area. One was the Chairman of the AUCCTU Presidium. Until 1975 this post was held by Aleksandr Shelepin, a powerful figure because of his concurrent membership in the CPSU Politburo and his previous position as head of the KGB, the huge Soviet intelligence service. After Shelepin's fall from power, the top Soviet labor post was vacant for over a year until the selection of Aleksei Shibaev in November 1976. Like most of his predecessors, Shibaev had no previous experience in trade union work.[4] Trained as an engineer, Shibaev served as a provincial CPSU Party Secretary, and had become a member of the CPSU Central Committee in 1961. At the time of his appointment Shibaev was a relatively obscure political figure with little knowledge of foreign affairs.

Shibaev served as Chairman of the AUCCTU Presidium until March 1982, when he was replaced by Stepan Shalayev, who previously served as Minister of the Timber and Paper Industry. Unlike any AUCCTU Chairman since Tomsky in the 1920s, Shalayev does have considerable prior labor experience. He was head of the Timber and Paper Workers' "Union" from 1963 until 1968, and then was appointed to the Secretariat of the AUCCTU. In March 1981 Shalayev was made a candidate member of the CPSU Central Committee. Although not considered a political heavyweight, his prior experience in labor work was an advantage not enjoyed by his predecessors.

Another key man in Soviet international labor work in the 1970s was Piotr Pimenov, one of the Secretaries of the AUCCTU Presidium, to whom the AUCCTU's International Department had been reporting ever since the early 1960s. Pimenov had considerable international experience, having been a Secretary of the Soviet-controlled World Federation of Trade Unions (WFTU) in Prague and a frequent delegate to various international labor gatherings. In the late 1970s he was an elected worker-member of the ILO Governing Body. In May 1980, Pimenov died (replaced by Aleksandr Subbotin) leaving a major gap to be filled in the top decision-making team for

[4]Blair Ruble, *Soviet Trade Unions* (Cambridge: Cambridge University Press, 1981), p. 42.

Soviet international labor policy. That team, in sum, usually consists of some high CPSU leaders involved in foreign affairs (such as Suslov, Kirilenko, and Ponomarev in the late 1970s), the AUCCTU Chairman, one or more AUCCTU Secretaries, the head of the International Department (and the relevant section chief), and the Director of the Institute of the International Workers Movement (IMRD).

Apart from the KGB, the Ministry of Foreign Affairs, and similar organizations, the main body responsible for implementing policy is the AUCCTU. The AUCCTU is completely controlled by the Politburo, and—as was pointed out in Part One—it unswervingly follows the Party's directives as articulated by the national labor authorities.[5] Just how the AUCCTU decides on methods of implementation is not at all clear. Edwin Morrell has pointed out that, in contrast to other subject matter in which the AUCCTU Presidium and Secretariat have implemented Politburo directives, foreign policy decisions appear to be made outside the usual channels. There appears to be almost no discussion of such decisions in plenums, and they are not discussed in either the bulletins or "protocol" pamphlets of the Presidium or the Secretariat. Conceivably, the AUCCTU Presidium and Secretariat have been making the decisions, but they have been restrictively classified and not distributed through the normal (but already restrictively distributed) bulletins and "protocol" pamphlets.[6] It is possible that the key decisions on policy implementation are made elsewhere, perhaps in the CPSU Secretariat and/or the intelligence services.

In any event, within the AUCCTU there is a major department concerned with executing Politburo directives. The International Affairs Department is one of the largest in the AUCCTU. It has a professional staff of about 100 divided along

---

[5]On CPSU control of AUCCTU, see Edwin Morrell, *Communist Unionism, Organized Labor and the Soviet State* (unpublished Ph.D. thesis, Harvard University, 1965); Thomas Lowit, *Le Syndicalisme de Type Sovietique* (Paris: Armand Collin, 1971); Joseph Godson, "The Role of the Trade Unions," in Leonard Schapiro and Joseph Godson, eds., *The Soviet Worker*, (New York: St. Martin's Press, 1981).

[6]Morrell, *op. cit.*, pp. 522–535.

geographical, and to some extent functional, lines.[7] There are specialists divided into a number of sections, including (a) Western Capitalist States, (b) Middle East and Africa, (c) Asia, (d) Latin America and the Caribbean, and (e) International Organizations. There are also international affairs "advisors" both to the AUCCTU Secretariat and to the International Affairs Department. For example, the current head of the International Affairs Department was listed only as an advisor until he became Director in 1975.

In addition to the International Affairs Department, a number of other departments have two or three specialists concerned with foreign relations. Many industrial departments— for example, the agricultural workers—have specialists concerned with foreign unions in their industries. (A few American unions also have one or two international affairs specialists). The Higher Trade Union School also has a Research Section with four or five foreign affairs specialists. This school, which now is housed in one of the best buildings in Moscow, employs a number of specialists to teach foreign trade unionists selected to study in Moscow. (From 1961 through the mid-1970s about 3,300 foreign unionists from 75 countries studied there, and about 1,000 received diplomas after completing its ten-month course.)[8] In addition, it should be noted that there is also a completely separate AUCCTU department, with a staff of seven to ten professionals, concerned with the labor organizations of ruling communist parties. The Higher Trade Union School also has another special faculty for students from these countries. From 1973 to 1976 over 1,300 "trade unionists" from Soviet bloc countries apparently attended this school.[9]

---

[7]By way of contrast, the AFL-CIO International Affairs Department has a professional staff of six.

[8]J. Svetlicnij, "At Moscow, A University for Trade Unionists from All Over the World," *World Trade Union Movement*, October 1976, pp. 30–31; and *Flashes*, September 10, 1975. *World Trade Union Movement* is a monthly, and *Flashes* a biweekly, publication of the WFTU.

[9]*Flashes*, October 13, 1976. Based on WFTU sources there does not appear to have been a significant change in recent years.

To implement policy, Moscow also can call on the centralized labor/political institutions in Eastern Europe and Cuba, the World Federation of Trade Unions (WFTU) in Prague, and Moscow-oriented communist parties, particularly in Europe. While there may be differences on some subjects between the Eastern European and Cuban communist leadership on one hand and the Soviet leadership on the other, there are few discernible differences in labor-related activities among these Moscow-oriented communist parties (with the exception of Poland in 1980–1982). In policy, in votes at international labor forums, and in general activities, the Soviets, East Europeans, and Cubans appear to be engaged in almost identical pursuits. This consensus and centralization provides the Kremlin with literally hundreds of additional international labor professionals, and numerous channels for training, influencing, and supporting foreign union leaders.

For example, in addition to the AUCCTU Higher Trade Union School for foreign trade unionists referred to above, over half a dozen training centers for foreign union leaders have been established in Eastern Europe since World War II. Although information on the centers is hard to come by, three major centers are the International Trade Union School in Prague, the Fritz Heckert Institute in Bernau, East Germany, and the Georgi Dimitrov Center in Sofia, Bulgaria. At the Bulgarian center alone, over 1,800 trade union functionaries from 60 countries had passed through the ten-month and shorter courses and seminars by 1977. The Bulgarian trade union newspaper *Trud* pointed to this training of labor cadres from Latin America, Africa, and Asia as an "extremely important manifestation of international and class solidarity."[10] In January 1976, the Cubans opened the Lazaro Peña national trade union school. In its first year the school offered two international courses for Latin Americans. The second course, which lasted for three months, was also attended by 50 "Angolan trade unionists."[11]

Just how the Soviets coordinate training programs with their

[10]BTA (Bulgarian News Agency), February 13, 1976.
[11]*Flashes*, October 13, 1976.

allies is uncertain. Like the AUCCTU, the Eastern European "trade unions" have active international affairs departments and sizeable staffs. There are periodic meetings of representatives of these bodies with their Soviet counterparts at Warsaw Pact and CMEA (Council on Mutual Economic Assistance) meetings, as well as at special meetings.[12] They also caucus at international labor gatherings. Perhaps the greatest number of contacts occurs at bilateral meetings between Soviet labor officials and representatives from individual bloc countries. Indeed, there is almost constant contact and interchange at every level. These meetings undoubtedly serve ritualistic purposes, but they are used to discuss substantive matters as well.

In spite of their differences with some nonruling communist parties, the Soviets also cooperate closely with a number of them in the labor field. Certainly in the past, for example, the Italian Communists were a major vehicle for Soviet activities in Africa; and today the French Communist Party and CGT are cooperating directly with the Soviets and the WFTU.[13]

The World Federation of Trade Unions (WFTU)

The WFTU is the most important Soviet-controlled international labor body. Essentially, it was created in 1945 to serve Soviet purposes after World War II and to eclipse most of the interwar international labor centers. In all likelihood the WFTU will continue to exist so long as it serves Soviet objectives.

With the exception of the American Federation of Labor, almost all significant communist and non-communist national centers joined the WFTU in the immediate postwar period. The Western international trade secretariats, however, also

[12]For a recent report on a "consultative meeting of national centers of the Socialist countries and the WFTU," see *ibid.*

[13]In Spring 1977, for example, the WFTU and the CGT center for aid to trade unions in the developing countries signed a cooperative agreement. The CGT, together with the WFTU, Soviet, and Eastern European centers, were also applauded by a number of Communist unions in Latin America and the Caribbean for their assistance at a meeting in Havana, Cuba. *Flashes*, May 4 and May 27, 1977. Based on recent WFTU publications, their close relationship with the CGT remained unchanged in 1983.

refused to become affiliated. (Unions in a given industry, such as transport workers, can join these industry-oriented international labor bodies called International Trade Secretariats, hereafter referred to as ITS.) Together with the AFL, their leaders believed that the WFTU was Soviet-controlled and would be used to support Moscow's political objectives. After the Kremlin tried to use the WFTU to disrupt the Marshall Plan and Western defense efforts, the non-communist Western centers withdrew in 1949 and joined with the AFL in creating the International Confederation of Free Trade Unions (ICFTU), abandoning the WFTU to Soviet dominance.[14] Since then, although Moscow has occasionally experienced some difficulty controlling the organization, particularly in the aftermath of the Soviet invasion of Czechoslovakia in 1968, the WFTU generally has served Soviet interests.

The WFTU claims to be the largest, and therefore the most representative, international labor federation. But while the WFTU claims that its affiliates have over 206 million individual members, it should be noted that the membership is derived almost exclusively from communist countries (over 130 million from the Soviet Union alone), where union membership is almost a necessity of life. The membership figures from twenty to thirty non-communist countries, which comprise five to ten percent of the WFTU affiliation, are very difficult to verify and almost certainly exaggerated.[15] Under these circumstances, membership figures cannot be considered very significant. With the exception of the communist bloc, and one or two Western exceptions such as France, the WFTU is relatively small—approximately five percent of workers affiliated with trade unions.

The WFTU also has created eleven international industrial labor bodies, or trade union internationals (TUIs), constituted from national unions affiliated with the WFTU, which are the

---

[14]For detailed analysis of this early postwar period, see Roy Godson, *op. cit.*; and Morton Schwartz, *Soviet Policies in the WFTU* (unpublished Ph.D. thesis, Columbia University, 1963).

[15]John P. Windmuller, *International Trade Union Movement* (The Netherlands: Kluwer, 1978), p. 90.

WFTU's counterparts to the previously mentioned ITS. But unlike the ITS, they are in reality funded by and subordinate to the WFTU's governing bodies. They present to the Kremlin another vehicle to influence industrial unions not affiliated with the WFTU.

The internal government of the WFTU may correspond to the standard pattern for international labor federations—a quadrennial Congress, a 33- to 35-member Executive Bureau, and an approximately 100-member General Council—but in reality, the locus of power lies elsewhere.[16] The WFTU's archives are not open to Western scholars; but it would appear that the key policymakers within the organization are the President, the Vice Presidents, and the Secretariat, composed of a General Secretary and seven Secretaries. Although the men who hold these positions represent various countries and continents (for example: the President is Hungarian, the Vice Presidents are Indian, Beninese, Czech, Lebanese, Cuban, and Cypriot, the General Secretary is Sudanese, and the Secretaries are Soviet, Czech, Chilean, Indian, and Polish), the Kremlin appears to control the organization completely.

To be sure, the Soviets have had difficulties from time to time persuading all the affiliates and the Secretariat of the "correctness" of Soviet policy and the Soviet concept of the organization. In 1968, for example, a major flap occurred in the WFTU as a result of the Soviet invasion of Czechoslovakia. The Communist Parties of France and Italy openly opposed the invasion, members of those two parties happened to occupy the posts of WFTU President and General Secretary at the time. The two men sent a joint letter of protest to the Communist Parties of all the nations participating in the invasion, and the WFTU Secretariat then voted eight to one (the Soviet member being the one opposed) in favor of sending the letter.

The Soviets moved quickly and firmly to reestablish control over the WFTU. Fourteen days after the Secretariat meeting, leaders of Soviet bloc labor organizations met with the top officials of the WFTU, reluctantly agreeing to reconstitute the WFTU in harmony with Soviet policy. At the WFTU Congress

[16]*Ibid.*, pp. 91–92.

the next year, most of the WFTU Secretaries who had voted to condemn the Soviet invasion were replaced, forty percent of the WFTU staff were dismissed, and the Secretariat lost the power to issue statements in the name of the WFTU.[17]

Another challenge to Soviet control over the WFTU was mounted by the Italian Communist-dominated labor federation, the CGIL. In the late 1960s, the Italian Communists, for tactical political reasons, wanted the WFTU to become involved in nonpolitical trade union affairs. Indeed, the Italian Secretary proposed using the TUIs, especially their Eastern and Western European affiliates, for this very purpose. The Soviets reportedly were unhappy with this nonpolitical approach, and were especially upset at the prospect of Soviet and East European labor officials meeting as a group to discuss such questions as wage differentials, working conditions, and the problems of workers in the communist bloc.

The CGIL's next move came at the 1973 WFTU Congress which approved the CGIL's proposal to create a new "associate membership" status in the WFTU, to which the CGIL shifted the next year when it joined the predominantly noncommunist European Trade Union Confederation (ETUC). The Soviets had hoped that granting the CGIL associate membership status, and thus greater autonomy within the WFTU, would placate the Italians. The Italians, in order to appeal to the Western Europeans in the ETUC, also wanted to distinguish themselves from the WFTU. Hence in 1978, calling the WFTU "a useless and outdated instrument," the CGIL left the WFTU completely.[18]

In spite of these occasional difficulties, however, the Soviets have been able to manage the WFTU successfully. Several reasons account for this Soviet agility. First, they are usually very well informed about developments within the organization. Soviet citizens are assigned to all major departments, and key officials or deputies are often Soviet citizens. In 1975, for example, a very experienced labor operator, Boris Averyanov, who headed the AUCCTU's Department of International Af-

[17]*Ibid.*, pp. 92–93, 101–103.
[18]*Ibid.*, pp. 103–104.

fairs for a number of years, was appointed to the WFTU Secretariat. Second, as will be discussed below, the Soviets reportedly provide the organization with almost all its funds. Indeed, according to a former high-ranking WFTU official, when Western affiliates complained that the disproportionately high number of Soviet and Warsaw Pact officials were unable to work effectively in Western countries (because they did not understand such things as collective bargaining), the Soviets responded that if the Western affiliates were dissatisfied they should pay for their own staff. Third, the Soviets and their allies, comprising well over half of the WFTU's affiliated membership, control enough votes to settle any issue in their favor. Usually, however, they prefer to avoid divisive votes at international meetings. Instead, they consult with, and if necessary pressure, affiliates prior to formal meetings to ensure that their policies are adopted without division. In the event that an affiliate is still reluctant to go along, CPSU officials sometimes will pressure the affiliate's parent communist party to guarantee compliance.

By virtue of the fact that they are well informed and have the votes, the funds, and leverage in the international communist movement, the Soviets have almost always managed to retain their control. When necessary, recalcitrant officials have been removed, and the WFTU has always fallen into line with basic Soviet policy on issues where initially there was disagreement, such as the Marshall Plan, the "expulsion" of the Chinese, and the European Economic Community.

To implement its decisions, the WFTU has a professional staff of approximately fifty officials in Prague, and several representatives in various parts of the world (e.g., Ernest de Maio, a former Vice President of the communist-controlled American union, the United Electrical Workers, was appointed in 1975 to represent the WFTU at the UN headquarters in New York.) There are geographic regional sections, and functional departments dealing with economic and social affairs, TUIs, publications, education, and international organizations. A new department to coordinate activities relating to multinational corporations was created in the 1970s, and in 1974, a committee of international labor scholars from nine member countries was established under the direction of Professor Baglai of Timofeiev's Institute on the International Workers Movement (IMRD). The major function of the committee, according to Baglai, was to coordinate research on economic and social trends that relate to the international labor movement, as well as to bring social scientists of "the most different tendencies" into contact with each other.[19]

The WFTU's main activities are: serving as a propaganda agency, amplifying Soviet themes, promoting trade union unity, providing political training to non-Western union leaders, and financially supporting favored unions. The organization engages in very few strictly trade union activities. It is basically political in orientation, although during the past few years it has shown more interest in economic and social affairs. Disseminating propaganda is one of its most important purposes, and the main targets are workers and union officials in the non-communist world.

A number of themes can be found in its monthly magazine *World Trade Union Movement*, which is translated into nine languages and disseminated throughout the world, as well as in WFTU radio programs and in the numerous propaganda conferences held in Europe and the non-Western world. Apart from stressing the achievements of the communist states (it maintains there are many) and the role of their unions (which, it says, have few, if any, problems), the organization's main emphasis is on the need for the worldwide unification of the labor movement.

The WFTU stresses that the "Socialist" states, their labor organizations, and the WFTU affiliates in the non-communist world are against all things that men fear most: economic insecurity, social injustice, exploitation, militarism, and war, particularly nuclear war. These themes are adapted to relate to contemporary issues and particular geographical regions. The campaign is designed to appeal to workers and union officials for whom opposition to global and regional evils is a worthwhile objective, regardless of who is promoting it. This

---

[19]*World Trade Union Movement*, March 1976, pp. 13–15.

often effectively blurs the distinction between communist and non-communist union leaders. After all, according to the propaganda, if the communists support such worthy goals, why should not communists as well as non-communists work and join together? Why should not trade unions throughout the world unite to promote these common aims?

Another major tactic of the WFTU's propaganda apparatus is to capitalize on clashes between the Third World and the West. Reacting to the Suez crisis in 1956, the Congo in 1961, the overthrow of Allende's regime in Chile in 1973, as well as apartheid in South Africa, the Arab-Israeli conflict, and the Falkland Islands war, the WFTU is quick to side with the position of Third World governments against, for the most part, that of Western countries. On the basis of these "common positions" and solidarity with the governments and the unions of the developing countries, the Soviets attempt to produce attitudes and consequences favorable to the Soviet bloc and damaging to the Western powers.

To further the momentum generated by its propaganda, the WFTU also promotes joint actions and other measures to "unify" communist and non-communist labor organizations on the international and regional levels, and to weaken and disintegrate the ICFTU and its regional organizations. Since the split in the international labor movement in the late 1940s and the creation of the democratic, Western-oriented ICFTU, the WFTU has continuously proposed to the ICFTU and the Christian democratic-oriented World Confederation of Labor (WCL) and their affiliates that "unity of action" would vastly increase the strength of the labor movement. (Organic unity of communist and non-communist international organizations is a long-range Soviet goal.) A 1975 WFTU General Council meeting reiterated this erstwhile point for what appeared to be the hundredth time. Noting that "encouraging results" have been achieved in bringing together national unions with different ideological affiliations, and that there had been progress in bringing about cooperation between the WFTU, the ICFTU, and WCL, the resolution stated that these results were still insufficient to bring the struggle of the workers to the level of present demands:

The WFTU considers that ideological differences do not present insurmountable obstacles; and that it is possible, while respecting each other's positions, to find ways toward an understanding which could lead to the creation of an international trade union center, grouping all the world's trade unions.[20]

The WFTU also frequently calls on the ICFTU and the WCL to join with it in supporting specific propaganda projects, such as the "defense of democracy in Portugal," support for the "anti-apartheid" movement, "justice for Palestinians," and almost any project that would lead non-communist unions away from working solely through the ICFTU and WCL.[21]

A major project along such propaganda lines was undertaken in the early 1980s to base efforts at "unity of action" specifically on the issue of "peace and disarmament". The communists took the initiative in organizing a World Trade Union Conference on the Social and Economic Aspects of Disarmament, held in Paris in December 1981. The final declaration adopted at the conference was intended to be "the basis for intensifying efforts in the struggle for peace . . . and for expanding cooperation between trade unions of different orientations."[22]

At the 10th WFTU Congress held in February, 1982, the Commission on Peace and Disarmament concluded that "trade unions in all countries should observe a "Month of Action for Disarmament" in June 1982.[23] The disarmament section of the basic document adopted by the WFTU Congress, blamed the transnational corporations for playing the decisive role in the Reagan Administration's decision to build and stockpile neutron weapons, and in NATO's plan to install new U.S. nuclear

---

[20]*World Trade Union Movement*, November 1975, p. 12.

[21]On the relative success of the Soviets and the WFTU in their efforts to unify the three international centers, see John P. Windmuller, "Realignment In The ICFTU: The Impact of Detente," *British Journal of Industrial Relations*, 1976, pp. 247–260.

[22]See *Flashes*, January 11, 1982, p. 1; Report of the Commission on Peace and Disarmament, *Appeal and Resolutions*, 10th World Trade Union Congress, WFTU, Havana, 1982, pp. 39–40.

[23]*Ibid.*, p. 40.

missiles in Europe. The basic document noted that "in spite of the differences and contradictions existing . . . among trade union organizations . . . they can find an objective common platform against imperialism in defense of the workers' basic interests, and peace is one such interest."[24]

The following month, in March 1982, the 17th Congress of the Soviet AUCCTU took up the theme of basing unity-of-action appeals on the peace and disarmament issue:

> The AUCCTU . . . must continue to struggle to develop unity of action of all countries' working people and trade unions in the struggle to avert the threat of war, to end the arms race, and to achieve disarmament. . . . A most important task of trade unions is to activate working people's mass anti-war demonstrations, to create a barrier in the way of the deployment of new American nuclear missile systems in the West European countries. . . . Soviet trade unions will seek to strengthen cooperation with social democratic and Christian trade unions on questions of preventing war and defending peace.[25]

The WFTU, unlike the ICFTU, was reluctant from its inception to sponsor regional organizations, perhaps because of what one writer has called the "efficiency of centralized administration" under Soviet direction, and because it feared losing control.[26] Unencumbered by a regional structure (perhaps with the exception of CPUSTAL, discussed below), however, the WFTU has had little difficulty entering into frequently cooperative relations with several autonomous regional trade union bodies in the non-Western world.

During the 1950s and the 1960s, several of these regional bodies appeared in African and Asian countries which wanted to project their nationalist ambitions onto the international labor movement. Declaring a desire to be independent from the

[24]*Trade Unions and the Challenges of the 1980s*, Main Document adopted by the 10th World Trade Union Congress, WFTU, Havana, 1982, pp. 15–16.
[25]"Resolution of the 17th U.S.S.R. Trade Union Congress on the AUCCTU Report", *Trud*, Moscow, March 21, 1982, pp. 304, as translated in FBIS, March 30, 1982, pp. R12–R14.
[26]John P. Windmuller, *Labor Internationals*, New York State School of Industrial and Labor Relations, Cornell University, 1969, p. 37.

three major international labor bodies, they encouraged their affiliates to withdraw from the global internationals, which in fact meant withdrawal from the ICFTU, as very few non-Western movements had been attached to the WFTU.

The WFTU, of course, encouraged this "anti-imperialist" move, and entered into friendly and cooperative relations with these bodies. The first was the International Confederation of Arab Trade Unions (ICATU). Founded with the professed aim of furthering pan-Arab unity and promoting socioeconomic development, the organization was created on the initiative of the Egyptian government. Up through the middle 1970s the requirements of "unity" and "economic and social advancement" were by and large determined by the Egyptians, although trade union bodies from sixteen Arab countries were affiliated with the ICATU.[27] Egypt, in the interest of unity, advocated cooperation with the WFTU. In 1969, for example, a WFTU-ICATU Standing Working Committee was created to coordinate "joint and similar activities," and four years later the WFTU characterized the cooperative relationship as having "developed continuously."[28] During these years the WFTU used the Standing Committee as a means of access in the Arab world for pro-Soviet propaganda stressing the themes of opposition to colonialism, "neoimperialism," and "Zionism." Even after Egyptian President Sadat terminated Egypt's close ties to the U.S.S.R. in 1976, relations between the ICATU and the WFTU remained friendly.

When Egypt concluded a separate peace agreement with Israel in 1979, Egypt became a virtual outcast from the Arab group of nations, and this ostracism was reflected in labor affairs. The other Arab countries forced the Egyptians out of

---

[27]It should be noted, however, that in the early 1970s about half of ICATU's affiliates, the "trade unions" in Iraq, Syria, North Yemen, South Yemen, Kuwait, and the PLO labor organizations, also became members of the WFTU.

[28]See the report on the 6th ICATU Congress in *World Trade Union Movement*, May 1976, p. 20. For a discussion of the origin and early relationship between ICATU and the WFTU, see Willard A. Beiling, *Pan-Arabism and Labor* (Cambridge, Mass.: Harvard University Press, 1960). See also George E. Lichtblau, "The Communist Labor Offensive in Former Colonial Countries," *Industrial and Labor Relations Review*, April 1961, pp. 376–401.

ICATU and transferred its headquarters from Cairo to Damascus. Subsequently a split occurred in ICATU, with the more conservative labor movements in Kuwait and Jordan sponsoring another branch of ICATU, with headquarters in Kuwait. This division continued into the early 1980s.

After 1978, with the more radical Arab nations dominating the main branch of ICATU located in Syria, the ICATU moved closer than ever to WFTU and Soviet positions. By the early 1980s the ICATU was notably to the left of the Arab League, even though the league is comprised primarily of the same governments which control the labor movements in ICATU. Soviet satisfaction with this leftist tilt in ICATU was manifest in WFTU General Secretary Zakaria's report to the 1982 WFTU Congress, in which he noted that, "For many years now we have had excellent relations of cooperation with the ICATU. We have a permanent Joint Working Committee which meets regularly twice a year." Zakaria protrayed the Committee as a means for coordinating WFTU and ICATU activities on issues of mutual agreement.[29]

Another organization used by the Soviets and the WFTU was the All-African Trade Union Federation (AATUF). Created in 1961 by the more "radical" labor figures in Africa (the Casablanca group), this organization, like ICATU, supported regional "unity," denounced "imperialism" and "colonialism," and basically reflected the approach of the radical nationalist regimes of Africa, particularly that of Kwame Nkrumah's Ghana. From its founding until the overthrow of Nkrumah in 1966, the organization's headquarters were in Accra, its Secretary General was a Ghanaian, and the bulk of its funds came from Nkrumah's "contingency funds." Although AATUF officially was unaligned, it worked closely with the WFTU and AUCCTU, overtly and covertly. Original letters and documents published by the Ghanaian unions after the fall of Nkrumah not only demonstrate the way in which he manipulated the organization to subvert what he regarded as hostile (pro-Western) foreign trade unions and governments,

---

[29]Ibrahim Zakaria, Report to the 10th World Trade Union Congress, Prague, 1981, p. 47.

but also the form and even the covert techniques that were employed by Soviet bloc operatives to support the organization.[30]

The Soviets had for some reason reduced their subsidy to AATUF, and the organization deteriorated in the late 1960s, even before the fall of Nkrumah. In the mid-1970s most African trade union centers joined the Organizations of African Trade Union Unity (OATUU), formed under the aegis of the government-level Organization of African Unity in 1973. The WFTU at first maintained that the new organization was a tool of "the imperialists and their reformist vassals" to prevent trade union unity on the African continent. In the spring of 1975, however, WFTU's attitude began to change. By August 1976, a WFTU delegation visited the OATUU Secretariat in Accra and signed an agreement "establishing practical cooperation between the two organizations."[31]

This cooperation has continued into the early 1980s. Like ICATU, the OATUU is well to the left of its parent body, in this case the OAU, and the ICATU and OATUU in fact held a joint meeting in 1982 to show "solidarity with the peoples of Palestine, Namibia, and South Africa." The WFTU provides some financial subsidies to the OATUU, and expressed satisfaction in 1982 with the "active cooperation" between the two organizations.[32]

In Latin America, the situation is a little different. Owing to dissimilar historical development patterns, many of the unions in the region have been affiliated loosely with one of the regional bodies of the three global internationals, ICFTU, WCL, and WFTU. The Soviet bloc's current regional body is the Permanent Committee for Labor Unity in Latin America

---

[30]See B. A. Bentum, *Trade Unions in Chains: How Kwame Nkrumah destroyed free trade unions in Ghana and attempted to extend this on the African continent*, Trade Union Congress of Ghana, Accra, December 1966. See also G. E. Lynd, *The Politics of African Trade Unionism* (New York: Praeger, 1968), pp. 163–171. Lynd is the pseudonym of George E. Lichtblau (see note 28), who for a number of years was the State Department's intelligence expert on the international labor movement.

[31]*World Trade Union Movement*, August 1975, pp. 8–9; and *World Trade Union Movement*, September 1976, pp. 8–9.

[32]Ibrahim Zakaria, Report to the 10th World Trade Union Congress, Prague, 1981, p. 47.

(CPUSTAL). Nominally independent of the Soviet bloc and WFTU, CPUSTAL has had a very difficult time surviving as an organization. Founded in Brazil in 1964, the organization originally established its headquarters in Chile. The 1973 Pinochet coup left CPUSTAL without a home, and its leaders did not want to be explicitly categorized as communist by basing the organization in Cuba. After a series of moves, CPUSTAL headquarters found a permanent home in early 1978 in Mexico City.

During the 1960s, the communists dominated the labor movements in only three non-communist countries in Latin America—Chile, Uruguay, and Ecuador—and only the Ecuadorean CTE was formally affiliated to the WFTU. In the mid-1970s, the WFTU sought to gain more direct affiliations in Latin America and the Carribean, with some success. Naturally the Cuban CTC joined after Castro's alignment with the U.S.S.R. In Peru (the CGTP) and Colombia (the CSTC) communist labor confederations grew to proportions of national significance, and they are both now WFTU affiliates. Smaller communist federations were affiliated from other countries such as El Salvador (FUSS), Guatemala (FASGUA), and Panama (CNTP). By 1982 the WFTU thus had twenty-two Latin American affiliates.

In the late 1970s, the communists placed considerable emphasis on building up a third organizational tie to Latin American labor in order to supplement the regional CPUSTAL and the global WFTU. These were six regional organizations for communist-oriented unions in six professional fields: graphic arts, textiles, transport, commerce, construction, and foodstuffs. These regional bodies sponsored numerous conferences for Latin American workers in these fields, trying to attract participation by non-communist unions, in line with the communists' "unity of action" effort.

At the national level, in the late 1970s and the beginning of the 1980s, the unity of action principle led the communists to join in joint councils with other labor confederations for rallies and protest strikes against declining real wages for workers. In some countries these unity bodies were formed on the initiative of the communists and in others by democratic unions. Countries with joint councils included Colombia, Ecuador, Panama, and Guatemala.

In Asia, where a large number of communist parties either have remained neutral in the Sino-Soviet struggle or have sided with the Chinese, the WFTU has not been able to attach itself to any regional trade union body, and few Asian unions have affiliated directly to it (The Chinese have not been formally expelled from the WFTU, but for all practical purposes they have not been members since the mid-1960s.) But WFTU officials have stepped up their efforts at building a regional trade union body in the area.[33]

The WFTU is also used to train labor cadres throughout the world. While the Soviets and the East Europeans frequently have bilateral relationships, and bring non-Western "trade unionists" to the Soviet Union and Eastern Europe for training, the WFTU is often used to select foreigners for training where it would be politically unwise for the Soviets to be involved directly. The WFTU also conducts regional training programs in cooperation with either a regional labor body or a sympathetic trade union center.

In Arab or African countries, for example, an AUCCTU or Soviet Foreign Ministry or KGB official will select what they regard as promising union officials and offer them scholarships at one of the Soviet or East European schools. If, however, individuals in a given country find it politically uncomfortable to accept (perhaps because their government does not want too many people attending training programs in the Soviet Union), the WFTU could issue the invitation, or the WFTU could run a training program in the region, so that the local leaders would not have to travel to the Soviet Union.

Usually, the training—whether conducted in a Soviet-bloc school or at a regional seminar—is almost completely ideological and political. Unlike the foreign labor education projects

---

[33]On the WFTU's analysis of trends in the region and efforts at organizing a regional body, see *World Trade Union Movement*, January 1977, pp. 14,17.

of the AFL-CIO, for example, little or no attention is devoted to the rudiments of organizing, negotiation, collective bargaining, and grievance procedures—the basic bread and butter concerns of unionists. Rather, they are designed to improve the propaganda skills and orientation, as opposed to the technical skills, of the student. Based on the reports of former instructors and students in these schools, a three- or ten-month course in the Soviet Union would include several months of Russian language and literature, Soviet history, "political economy," philosophy, and "scientific communism," the history of the international labor movement, and bookkeeping.[34]

A somewhat similar curriculum (with perhaps less emphasis on the Soviet Union and without language training) is taught at regional WFTU schools. The program generally will also be tailored to apply to the particular region or industry, especially if it is conducted under the auspices of a TUI or a particular WFTU Department. These seminars are organized in one or more parts of the world almost on a monthly basis.

For example, a report on a four-day textile industry seminar in Quito, Ecuador, organized by the Textile TUI with the collaboration of the communist-oriented Ecuador Confederation of Labor (CTE), and with the participation of CPUSTAL, the ILO, and a fraternal delegation of AUCCTU textile workers, stated that sixty-two delegates from ten Latin American countries attended. After discussing the working environment of textile, clothing, leather, fur, and shoe workers, and the implementation of ILO conventions on freedom of association, "the participants noted that in all Latin American countries, except the Socialist Republic of Cuba, the working environment was harmful to workers' health and in some cases unsuitable for human beings, which in addition to exploitation

---

[34]Interviews with former AUCCTU instructors who have emigrated, and interviews with former Moroccan, Egyptian, and Palestinian "students" in the Soviet Union and Eastern Europe. A brief history and description of these activities can also be found in *Afro-Asian Labor Bulletin*, March 1972, published by the National Trade Union Congress of Singapore. For a recent report on training at a Hungarian center, see "From Propaganda Mill to Textile Mill: A First Hand Account of Indoctrination," in *Workers Under Communism*, No. 4, Fall 1983, pp. 17–21.

by imperialism and monopolism, daily worsened their working conditions."[35] Another report noted that the WFTU and the Fiji Council of Trade Unions organized a seminar attended by thirty-two representatives from five trade union organizations from Fiji, Australia, New Caledonia, and East Timor. The main topic was "Labor Versus Capital." "Various lecturers gave courses on the role of trade unions, the multinational companies, the international trade union movement, and unity."[36]

Labor education courses offered by communist unions within one country appear to be somewhat more practical than the propagandistic offerings in the Soviet-bloc schools and the WFTU's regional seminars. For example, in 1982 one communist national confederation in Latin America planned to offer local courses on labor press and public relations, teaching methods, collective bargaining, and industrial safety, in addition to the more highly political topics of "the international labor movement," and "unity of action."

Based on figures supplied by the Soviets and East Europeans as well as by the WFTU, in the mid-1970s approximately 2,000 trade union officials from non-Western countries were attending courses from three to ten months duration each year, with approximately the same number attending regional seminars (usually sponsored by the WFTU and lasting from several days to two weeks).[37] Reporting specifically on those courses which the WFTU helped organize directly, WFTU General Secretary Zakaria noted that between 1974 and 1978 there were 34 national and 9 regional seminars with a total participation of 1,928 trade unionists. The scope of the WFTU's training program expanded considerably during the next four years (1978–1981), with 63 national seminars, 20 regional seminars, and a total of 4,576 participants.[38]

The Soviets began these sizeable training programs modestly

[35]*Flashes*, September 3, 1976.
[36]*Flashes*, September 24, 1976. For reports on WFTU training programs in Africa, see *Flashes*, September 10, 1976.
[37]See, for example, *Flashes*, December 7, 1976.
[38]Ibrahim Zakaria, Report to the 10th World Trade Union Congress, WFTU, Prague, 1981, p. 24.

in the late 1960s, and gradually expanded them. It would appear that up to 1977 approximately 15,000 non-Western officials attended courses in the Soviet Union and Eastern Europe, and another 10,000 to 15,000 participated in the much shorter programs in their respective regions. As far as can be determined, however, these training programs are not used directly to train local leaders in how to conduct political strikes, engage in espionage, or in *coups d'etat*. But it is quite possible that these educational activities may be used to identify cadres for this special type of training, or as a method of providing cover for an individual who undergoes such training.

Another technique used by the WFTU is financing foreign trade unions. Very little information is available on these matters. The Soviets and the WFTU do not usually publish financial statements. Moreover, according to a former high-ranking WFTU official, a small committee comprised of Soviet officials and the General Secretary meet in private to allocate these funds. Based on a few pieces of information and some reasonable calculations, however, it is possible to draw some conclusions about the organization's financial support of foreigners. One of the best indications of WFTU activities in this area came in the 1960s. Cornell Professor John P. Windmuller published "hard" data which indicated that the WFTU had an International Solidarity Fund that spent $1.3 million during a 42-month period between January 1, 1962, and June 30, 1965. A breakdown of this annual budget of approximately $325,000 indicated that 60 percent went into trade union support in non-Western areas; 25 percent was spent in support of "national liberation" struggles; and about 15 percent went to support strikes and other forms of conflict in unspecified areas.[39]

Although, as Professor Windmuller and others have pointed out, the WFTU appeared to suffer from a major shortage of funds in the mid-1960s, by mid-1970s this no longer appeared to be true, judging from the increased rate of its publications and activities.[40] In 1980, the U.S. government estimated the

[39]Windmuller, *Labor Internationals*, pp. 35–36.
[40]Windmuller, *International Trade Union Movement*, p. 93.

WFTU's annual budget at about $8 million, most of it spent on publications, meetings, conferences, etc.[41]

Unfortunately, more comprehensive figures are not available, although there are occasional reports of WFTU grants to trade unions in various countries.[42] In addition, because many of the small communist-run national centers in Latin America and Africa receive almost no money in dues, it is not unreasonable to conclude that they are receiving a major portion of their limited funds in subsidies from the Soviet bloc and the WFTU. Otherwise, it is difficult to see how they could survive on an operational basis, let alone send representatives to international meetings.

The WFTU also has some potential use as a vehicle for promoting or coordinating political strikes. In the late 1940s, the Russians tried to use the organization in conjunction with European Communist Parties to direct political strikes against the Marshall Plan and Western defense efforts. By and large, this effort failed, largely due to the transnational coalition of non-communist European and American trade unionists and Western governments.[43] Since that time, the WFTU and the TUIs have occasionally tried to organize or join in international political strikes or boycotts. Usually these initiatives have been ineffective, mainly because non-communist union leaders refused to take part in national or international political strikes on issues which were not considered vital to their immediate interests.

A WFTU effort in the late 1970s to encourage maritime and dock workers throughout the world to boycott Chilean ships also failed, in spite of the militance of maritime workers and the near-universal condemnation of the Pinochet regime in trade union circles. If, however, increasing numbers of trade

---

[41]Central Intelligence Agency, *Soviet Covert Action and Propaganda*, printed in *Soviet Covert Action (The Forgery Offensive)*, Hearings before the Subcommittee on Oversight of the Permanent Select Committee on Intelligence, House of Representatives, February 6 and 19, 1980 (Washington, D.C.: U.S. Government Printing Office, 1980), p. 79. The study estimated that the WFTU had a staff of only thirty.
[42]For example, the *Nigerian Herald* of April 23, 1976 reported that the WFTU had given the Nigerian TUC $30,000.
[43]See Roy Godson, *op. cit.*

unionists fall under communist influence, it will become much easier for the WFTU to promote political strikes. As both American agribusiness and the Ford Administration discovered in 1975 when dock workers refused to handle Soviet-bound grain, these strikes can be very disruptive in modern integrated economies.

One issue area, ostensibly nonpolitical, on which the WFTU has focused increasing attention is the impact of multinational companies on labor. This concern in itself is not unusual. Both national and international trade unions have felt increasingly threatened by these giant conglomerates, and have devoted a great deal of their energy to studying and trying to deal with them. The WFTU, however, has a somewhat different perspective on this issue. Unlike most non-communist union organizations, it does not accept their existence, and does not believe that international codes of conduct and the creation of countervailing trade union power are what is basically required to deal with the new multinational methods of production.[44] Instead, Soviet-oriented trade unionists see these companies as simply another manifestation of capitalist society which must be destroyed. Reform will not save or really improve that society or its corporations. The WFTU believes in strong national control of the economy—basically nationalization, with the national labor movement playing a major role in controlling the nationalized firms. But the communists—and in this they are joined by non-communists—believe workers should cooperate across state boundaries to protect their interests.

For the WFTU, however, cooperation across state boundaries means breaking down the barriers between communist and non-communist organizations, and then "coordinating" international labor activities to "defend" worker interests. The

---

[44]The report of the Commission on Transnational Corporations (TNCs) at the 1982 WFTU Congress noted that "efforts to draw up a 'Code of Conduct' for the TNCs have not made progress. Moreover the TNCs and their home governments virtually ignore the existing international instruments. . . . The implementation of these documents requires the most intense trade union activity. . . ." *Appeal and Resolutions.* 10th World Trade Union Congress, WFTU, Havana, 1982, p. 44.

latter, of course, refers to more than an exchange of information and the multinational coordination of trade union bargaining strategy. It refers to manifestations of international solidarity, including the coordination of international strikes. Of course, the operations of Western multinationals in Eastern Europe and the Soviet Union are excluded from this category of actions. The WFTU has maintained that "action against the multinational companies is a question of class struggle in the capitalist countries."[45]

Just how the WFTU and its affiliates can coordinate international solidarity is uncertain. Certainly the WFTU is appealing to workers of all persuasions to break down the barriers set up by the "reactionary" forces and to work together to deal with the new threat. When this appeal is restricted to cooperation between communist and non-communist unions dealing with the same company in different countries, or in international organizations such as the EEC, it is quite powerful. (How else can trade unions dealing with the Ford Motor Company or the Dunlop Tire Company gain sufficient unity and strength to influence the outcome of negotiations? Or how else can the workers in the European metal industry influence the EEC's regulations pertaining to multinationals unless they cooperate?) Whether the argument will be powerful enough, however, remains to be seen.

Moreover, even if there is united action of some kind, coordinating and sustaining international strikes is no easy matter. Given the resources and dedication of the WFTU and communist union leaders, international strikes may become a problem in the future. In the 1970s however, few instances of multinational bargaining, much less strikes, occurred. More-

[45]For a comparison of the various international views on multinationals, see Everett M. Kassalow, "Attitudes towards the Multinationals," *Free Labor World*, June 1976, pp. 4–7. For a succinct statement by a WFTU official, see the interview with Pierre Baghi, *Flashes*, April 7, 1976.

It should also be pointed out that despite their public opposition to the multinationals, the Soviets and Eastern Europeans have dramatically increased their cooperation with these companies. See, for example, "Coping with Multinationals," AFL-CIO *Free Trade Union News*, December 1976.

over, few if any involved cooperation between communist and non-communist unions.[46] Nevertheless, the WFTU has been taking the problem of the multinationals seriously. In 1976 the Secretariat took a number of steps to improve its ability to deal with multinationals. Then-Secretary Akis Fantis was given responsibility for matters bearing on the subject, a standing working committee was established, and "a special WFTU body for trade union work in connection with these companies" was also created.[47]

In 1982 the 10th Congress of the WFTU called for the WFTU Commission on Transnational Corporations (TNCs) to work closely with the WFTU's Trade Union Internationals to strengthen their work of maintaining close contact among unions at the plant, regional, national, and international levels which confront the same multinational corporation. Through these contacts, the unions concerned should target the most important multinational firms, collect and distribute information about them, set up a Coordinating Committee of workers employed by the same multinational, promote research on the problem of the multinationals, and work in the UN and the ILO to counteract the corporations.

In keeping with the new emphasis on peace and disarmament efforts as the basis for trade union unity of action, the WFTU Congress noted that as "an integral part of the military-industrial complex, the dominant TNCs accelerate the nuclear arms race, thus constituting a threat to world peace, not only because of the super-profits earned from arms production, but also because these military means are used to buttress their economic domination and the plundering of nations."[48]

Exactly how all the WFTU's activities are financed remains a mystery. Most likely the money comes from either the affiliates or directly from their governments. As over seventy per-

---

[46]See Herbert R. Northrup and Richard L. Rowan, *Multinational Collective Bargaining Attempts* (Industrial Research Unit, University of Pennsylvania, Philadelphia, 1979), pp. 533–534, 542.

[47]*Flashes*, March 17, 1976.

[48]Report of the Commission on Transnational Corporations, in *Appeal and Resolutions*, 10th World Trade Union Congress, WFTU, Havana, 1982, pp. 43–44.

cent of the affiliated membership comes from the Soviet Union and the Eastern bloc, it seems probable that the bulk of the funds originates in these countries, especially since the affiliates in Western Europe and the Third World are for the most part rather poor.[49] Whether the money comes in the form of dues or contributions from affiliated labor organizations, or whether is it derived from government grants is, of course, unimportant. Clearly, the authorizing agents are the Soviet and European communist parties. Both the size and expenditure of the WFTU's regular administrative budget and its international solidarity fund are determined ultimately by the national party/government officials.

Soviet leaders derive a number of advantages from their control of the WFTU. Indeed it is a vehicle that would be difficult to replace. It is a channel for assisting legal and illegal communist parties and trade unions. It also provides the Soviet bloc with access to a variety of non-communist organizations. It gives them a cloak of credibility that they would have difficulty obtaining independently, even though many people are aware that the Kremlin dominates the organization. The WFTU also helps them to weaken and reduce the appeal of the ICFTU and the ITS, the major international labor bodies in the non-communist world.

The WFTU also has its limitations, however. It is not always easy to control. The Soviets have had, and to some extent continue to have, difficulty in giving direction to some of their European affiliates and associates. The WFTU is viewed by many in the non-communist world as an anachronistic political organization that serves relatively little purpose, and has on occasion been a hindrance to Soviet activities. For these reasons, the Soviets have developed their own bilateral relations with unions in the non-communist world, particularly since the late 1960s. In this way, they are not forced to rely on the WFTU, and can appeal to unions which are reluctant to work with the organization. If the day comes when the

---

[49]A former WFTU official thinks the French CGT may have contributed to the WFTU, but he believes that except for token symbolic contributions the only other large Western affiliate, the Italian CGIL, has not.

WFTU appears to be a net liability, the Soviets will have other vehicles at their disposal.

Changing the Global Balance

Europe. In recent years, the Soviets have not attempted to use European labor to bring a communist party to power, particularly in central and northern Europe. Rather, efforts have been made to use labor to support detente, reduce Western defense efforts, weaken the region economically, and especially to increase the political influence of Moscow-oriented communists. Further development of political influence might enable the Kremlin to use labor either to change the system of government in key West European countries, or to engage in sabotage and paramilitary activities in support of Soviet objectives.

The maintenance and exploitation of detente and Soviet "peace" themes are among the major activities of the Soviet international labor complex. The Soviets seek to use labor as a propaganda vehicle to influence European voters and politicians. Hardly a month goes by without a Soviet-influenced trade union statement or a demonstration against NATO decisions. In addition, a major part of the "peaceful coexistence" effort in the trade union area is devoted to the exchange of thousands of delegations and the publication of a multitude of declarations. The Soviets and their allies spend a great deal of energy and very large sums on exchanges. For example, Moscow reported in 1977 that whereas they exchanged several hundred delegations with 50 to 60 countries annually in the 1950s, they exchanged 1,500 delegations in 1974, over 1,700 in 1975, and by 1977 were issuing joint declarations or "actively cooperating" with trade unions in 128 countries.[50]

Over a five year period, from 1972 to 1977, Soviet labor organization exchanged a total of 9,500 delegations, and in the succeeding five years (1978–82) they continued to maintain a

---

[50]Morrell, *op. cit.*, pp. 562–567; "An AUCCTU Plenum," *Trud*, May 29, 1975; "U.S. Scored for Blocking U.S.S.R. Trade Union Delegation Visas," *Tass*, July 13, 1976, FBIS.

high level of activity, exchanging 8,300 delegations with 145 countries (having received 4,600 and sent 3,700).[51] In West Germany particularly, the pace of exchanges has risen dramatically. In 1970, for example, some 50 West German and East European union leaders traveled back and forth; in 1974, the figure was over 400. The British have followed suit. In 1975 alone, over 30 delegations from British unions visited the Soviet bloc, and the Soviets and East Europeans sent almost as many delegations to the U.K.[52] Glowing accounts of these exchanges are printed in the Western commercial and labor press. (The East German news agency ADN, for example, quoted Jack Jones, the most important British union leader in 1976, as saying he had "felt at home" in the G.D.R.)

In addition, the Soviets and the WFTU organize propaganda conferences and seminars almost monthly. These very widespread and costly activities have helped make "detente" respectable in trade union and Socialist circles, and have helped to reduce European labor's interest in an anti-communist posture and in defense expenditures.

Second, the Soviets have used organized labor to augment strains and tensions in Western society, or what is sometimes referred to as "the contradictions of capitalism." In Europe, this has meant promoting economic difficulties as well as strengthening unions and communist parties that can take advantage of the "crisis" of capitalism. As was discussed, the Soviets view the increasing economic crisis in the West, which had been expected to appear sooner or later, as a favorable trend. Moreover, while they did not engineer the Arab oil embargo and subsequent price increases, they certainly encouraged the Arabs in these efforts.[53] At the same time, the increasing militance of workers in England, France, Italy, and elsewhere—who were hard hit by these developments—is seen as a natural defense of their interests in a capitalist economy,

---

[51]See Pimenov's article in *Trud*, May 21, 1977, and Shalayev's Report to the 17th U.S.S.R. Trade Union Congress, translated in FBIS, March 30, 1982, p. R17.

[52]*Economist Newspapers*, March 12, 1975, and July 7, 1976.

[53]See, for example, Robert O. Freedman, *Soviet Policy Toward the Middle East* (New York: Praeger, 1975), p. 140.

and is applauded. In other words, the Kremlin helped to increase the economic strains in the West not only by encouraging price increases by oil producers, but also by promoting trade union militance that in some cases is designed to hinder the "capitalist" economies still more.

Although the Kremlin today does not promote the immediate use of strikes to bring down Western economies and systems of government, it is not unreasonable to conclude that the Soviets move subtly in this direction whenever they forsee a momentary political payoff.[54] In Britain, the Soviets have contributed in a small way to the country's economic difficulties by encouraging both communist and non-communist trade union leaders to take advantage of unsettled industrial relations and hyperinflation. For example, during the 1970s a major tactic employed by the British Communists, supported by the Soviets, was to join with non-communists in trying to discredit the moderates, and to demand very high wage increases, frequently far above increases in the cost of living. As some of these very high wage claims were successful, the inflationary spiral was exacerbated and confidence in the British economy declined. When they failed, the communists blamed the moderate union officials and pushed for strikes, which also damaged the economy.

In France and Portugal, the Soviets encouraged the Communist Parties and the unions they controlled to engage in similar tactics. In Italy, the Soviets and the Italian Communists for a time encouraged militant strike actions "to defend the workers' interests." But when the Italian Communist Party in the mid-1970s sought sufficient political respectability in order to enter a coalition government, there was much less emphasis on high wage claims and strikes. Indeed, the Communist Party and the CGIL became conservative in their demands.

The Soviets also materially support trade union strike activities as well as favored labor organizations. It is impossible, of course, to ascertain the full extent of this support. Nevertheless, it is clear that they have assisted strike activities. On oc-

---

[54]Moscow also may not have been as active in this area due to a belief that such a policy might endanger detente.

casion, communist-bloc financial support for a labor movement has been acknowledged.[55]

Although there is some statistical evidence to indicate that communist parties and communist-controlled unions appear able to affect the prevalence of strike activity,[56] this should not be taken to mean that industrial strife and economic difficulties in Europe have been caused in the main by Moscow. Rather, it would be closer to the truth to suggest that the Soviets have been encouraging European Communists to take advantage of whatever forces are at work to increase Western economic and political difficulties.

The third approach Moscow employs in the trade union area is the promotion of "working class unity." For decades, the Kremlin has attached great importance to bringing Soviet labor organizations and communist-controlled unions in the West into the mainstream of the international labor move-

[55]Although it is impossible to determine the precise extent of Soviet financial support for European trade unions, the tip of what very well may be an iceberg can be seen. For example, according to Radio Moscow, August 11, 1972, Jimmy Reid, then Communist Secretary of the Scottish engineering workers, thanked the Soviet authorities for giving his union approximately $50,000 for strike actions. Cited in Brian Crozier, "Soviet Union's New Takeover Bid," *Forum World Features*, August 1973. In another Radio Moscow program, in January 1974, Leslie Dixon, a member of the Amalgamated Union of Engineering Workers Council, was quoted as saying that Soviet unions had made a substantial financial contribution to his union's "dispute fund." See Brian Crozier, "Soviet Interest in Industrial Unrest," *Soviet Analyst*, February 14, 1974. In another article, Crozier, then the Director of the Institute for the Study of Conflict, listed several of the main KGB, AUCCTU, and CPSU Secretariat officials who he maintained were helping to coordinate strikes in Great Britain. "New Light on Soviet Subversion (1)," *Soviet Analyst*, March 28, 1974.

Former Secretary of State Kissinger estimated that in a twelve month period, the Soviet Union sent $50 million to the Portuguese Communist Party. *New York Times*, April 18, 1975. Undoubtedly, some of these funds were used to help establish Communist control of the Portuguese national trade union center, Intersindical. Indeed, Fletcher School of Law and Diplomacy professor John Roche had a photostat of a telegram from the Soviet Bank for Foreign Trade to a Lisbon bank transferring $28,570 to the Intersindical. "The Portuguese Labyrinth II," *King Features*, August 26, 1975. Moreover, in a rare acknowledgement of organizational assistance, an East German labor leader stated that his organization has given the Portuguese unions one million escudos, and promised additional aid for union buildings, duplicating machinery, and so forth. "Voice of the GDR," August 2, 1974 (BBC, SWB, EE/4669/A1/1).

[56]Douglas Hibbs, *Industrial Conflict in Advanced Industrial Societies* (Cambridge, Mass.: Center for International Studies, Massachusetts Institute of Technology, April 1974).

ment, primarily to give them much greater access to labor and political forces in the West. The Soviets expect communists in the labor movement to become more influential as a result of this entree. Ultimately, they should be able to outmaneuver the non-communists and gain complete control of almost the entire trade union movement.

Although they made a number of attempts to recover from the splits of the late 1940s and to recapture the unity that was achieved in the early postwar period, the Soviets did not meet with much success until the early 1970s.[57] Specifically, in addition to the bilateral contacts they have now established with almost every European national center, they have successfully brought together the ICFTU's and WFTU's European affiliates under the umbrella of the ILO, and they are encouraging more meetings of this kind. (However, in November 1982, the ICFTU & the WCL called a halt to such meetings until the restrictions on *Solidarnosc* in Poland are lifted.)

The Soviets also have encouraged, and have been the beneficiaries of, efforts to unify the European labor movement on a pan-European basis. The Communist-dominated Italian central body, CGIL, on its withdrawal from the WFTU, was accepted into the European Confederation of Trade Unions (ETUC) in 1974. The French Communist CGT also applied for membership, so far without success. If it is admitted in the future, a move to bring in East European labor organizations can be expected.[58]

At the same time, the Soviets and the communist labor organizations in Western Europe have encouraged unity in the industrial internationals. The French Communist CGT Printers Union (Fédération Française du Livre) succeeded in gaining entry into the International Graphic Workers Federation.

---

[57]The best sources of information on trade union unification are polemical. The WFTU's monthly, *World Trade Union Movement*, carries at least one article on this subject almost every month. For a brief historical but critical analysis of Soviet policy, see Claude Harmel, *Est et Ouest*, March 1-15, 1975, pp. 12–24.

[58]On the origin and evolution of the ETUC, see John P. Windmuller, "European Regionalism: A new factor in international labor," *Industrial Relations Journal* (London), Summer 1976. On the relative success of the Soviets in Europe, see also Windmuller's "Realignment in the ICFTU: The Impact of Detente," *loc. cit.*

Communist unions have also been admitted into one or two European trade secretariats, such as the European Metal Workers Federation. In Southern Europe, they have also made considerable headway. In Italy, the three main national centers—the Communist CGIL, the predominantly Catholic CISL, and the Socialist Unione Italiana del Lavoro (UIL) (which broke away from the CGIL in the late 1940s)—have established joint organizations for close collaboration, a compromise, instead of concluding earlier moves for organic unification.

The Communist Party in Portugal, with Soviet support and assistance, captured control of the Portuguese central labor body, Intersindical, after the fall of the Salazar/Caetano dictatorship in 1974. Since then, however, the democratic labor forces have been fighting back, and by the early 1980s they had attained a significant minority position.

In Spain, a similar pattern appeared at first after the death of Francisco Franco in 1975. Working clandestinely, the Communists dominated the trade unions which appeared in embryonic form during Franco's last years in competition with his controlled "vertical" unions. When these new, independent unions came out in the open in 1977, the Communists maintained the largest share, winning 35 percent of the races for worker-delegates in 1978, more than any other political party. The democratic socialist unions worked hard to compete with the Communists, however. Two years later, in 1980, the Communists won only 31 percent. In contrast, the democratic socialists climbed from 22 percent in 1978 to 30 percent in 1980. Thus the Spanish Socialists achieved virtual parity with the Communists. In the 1982 round of elections for worker delegates, the two groups again were roughly equal.[59]

It should be noted that in the mid-1970s Moscow pushed hard for the entry of European Communist-controlled unions into the mainstream of the European labor movement in spite of the Kremlin's strained relationship with some of the major Western Communist Parties. Even in Italy, the most troublesome of the Parties from the Soviet point of view, Moscow and

[59]See "Las Otras Elecciones," *Cambio 16*, Madrid, September 13, 1982.

the WFTU lauded achievements toward unification on the national level in the mid-1970s, as well as the CGIL's admission into the ETUC. This occured in spite of the fact that in order to gain admission into the non-communist body, the CGIL transformed itself into an "associate" rather than an active member of the WFTU. Moscow seemed to believe that it was useful to strengthen the position of the European communists in the non-communist labor movement, even if it meant a weakening of one of their own fronts. This also would seem to indicate that the strain between the Soviet and Italian Parties, at that stage anyway, had not led Moscow to stop supporting what it regarded as important pro-Soviet forces on the continent. The costs of this policy to the Soviet position increased considerably with the total disaffiliation of the CGIL from the WFTU in 1978.

In line with their doctrine, the Soviets and the European Communist Parties also stress the development of communist strength in several sectors of the labor movement. They have placed considerable emphasis on building up communist strength among workers in (a) new service, engineering, and technological industries (the new strata resulting from the "scientific and technical revolution")—what in France would be referred to as the "cadres"; (b) migratory workers, who can play a role in their host country in northern Europe, as well as in southern Europe and North Africa when they return home; and (c) the military. Perhaps based on the experience of Chile and Portugal, the Soviets now are seeking the support, or at least the neutrality, of what Timofeiev refers to as "progressive military personnel," which he says is a "prerequisite" for the world revolution.[60]

---

[60]The WFTU and TUIs have placed particular emphasis on the first two sectors. See, for example, the Charter of Demands adopted by the WFTU's International Trade Union Conference of Engineers, Managerial Staffs, and Technicians, in *World Trade Union Movement*, November 11, 1975; and the "Charter of Trade Union Rights and Economic and Social Demands of the Workers in Capitalist Countries" adopted by the 8th WFTU Congress, Varna, 1973, in *Flashes*, May 26, 1976. The French, Italian, and small West German Communist Parties have also devoted considerable efforts to influence these sectors. It is more difficult to get information on the tactics that are used to penetrate the military.

Recent Soviet efforts to unify the communist and non-communist labor movements and gain control of various sectors, however, do not mean that the Soviets have been completely successful. While they have made considerable progress in the era of detente, Soviet and European Communists have not achieved full acceptance. The ICFTU as an institution still refuses to cooperate with the WFTU. The French CGT and the East Europeans have not been admitted into the ETUC. In Britain, leading communist union leaders have either been defeated in union elections or forced to disavow their party connection. Even in Italy, where the communists have been close to entering a government coalition, organic unity between communist and non-communist central labor bodies has not been achieved. Thus, while the Soviets have good reason to be pleased with their efforts at working class unity thus far, they still have a way to go toward realizing their ultimate goals.

The extent to which the Soviets have prepared or intend to use unions for paramilitary and espionage activities cannot be ascertained. Clearly, however, the Soviets are continuing to penetrate European unions. In West Germany, for example, in the mid-1970s the security services arrested several Soviet-bloc agents who held senior union posts. Whether these individuals are assigned only to obtain information or also to become "agents of influence" in a major institution is unclear, but the Soviets obviously believe it is worth doing. There are also indications that they are developing sabotage capabilities through their connections in Western unions. Presumably Western security services have an assessment of the bloc's capabilities and intentions, but only occasionally do tidbits of information on this subject come to light.[61]

It should be noted, however, that there may be a significant difference between the early postwar Soviet ability to manipulate European communist parties and trade unions and the

---

[61]For a discussion of the KGB department which handles this subject, and the example of the British expulsion in 1971 of 105 "diplomats," several of whom were accused of working with British unions and preparing for sabotage activities, see John Barron, *KGB* (New York: Reader's Digest Press, 1974), especially pp. 320–330.

current situation. Certainly the relationship has been complicated by a number of factors, such as detente, and the change of leadership and rapid turnover of party membership in Europe. What was never an easy task was certainly made more difficult by such developments. Moreover, some students of European communism and labor also suggest that the Italian and French parties no longer have complete control of the CGIL or CGT.[62]

Although the Soviets themselves maintain that they have not altered their goals or overall policy, a number of Western analysts maintain that there has been a fundamental policy shift, that detente is genuine. Others believe that the Soviet leaders, for a variety of domestic and international reasons, remain expansionist and are trying to weaken the West and increase their own power, although almost certainly they cannot manipulate even European communist-oriented unions as effectively as they did immediately after World War II.

These interpretations and actual Soviet activities in the labor field are similar in some important respects to those that

---

[62]Most observers believe that shortly after World War II, the major trade union centers in France and Italy fell under the control of Communist Parties subservient to Moscow. For discussion of the more complex subsequent relationships between the Soviets and the major European Communist Parties, see Donald M. Blackmer and Annie Kriegel, *The International Role of the Communist Parties of Italy and France* (Cambridge, Mass.: Center for International Studies, Harvard University, 1975); Donald M. Blackmer and Sydney Tarros, eds., *Communism in Italy and France* (Princeton: Princeton University Press, 1975); and Neil McInnes, *The Communist Parties of Western Europe* (London: Oxford University Press, 1975). By the mid-1970s some writers differed on the extent of Soviet and Communist Party control of the CGT and CGIL. See André Barjonet, *La CGT* (Paris: Seuil, 1968); the debate between Gerard Adam and Jean Ranger in *Revue Française de Science Politique*, June 1968, pp. 524–539, and December 1968, pp. 182–187; and Jean-Daniel Reynaud, "Trade Unions and Political Parties in France: Some Recent Trends," *Industrial Relations Review*, January 1975, pp. 208–226. Walter Kendall in *The Labor Movement in Europe* (London: Allen Lane, 1975) argued that the CGT and CGIL were then still controlled by the French and Italian Communist Parties; and the French journals *Les Études Sociales et Syndicales* and *Est et Ouest* provide detailed information to indicate that the CGT and CGIL were still controlled by Communist Parties basically loyal to Moscow. For an example of a commentator who believed that the CGIL was no longer an instrument of the Italian Communist Party, see Peter R. Weitz, "Labor and Politics in a Divided Movement," *Industrial and Labor Relations Review*, January 1975, pp. 226–243.

prevailed from 1945 to 1947. Then, too, there were two schools of thought about Soviet intentions and Moscow's efforts to promote peaceful coexistence and unify the labor movement. After 1947, when the Kremlin adopted much tougher tactics and overtly used labor to impede European recovery and defense efforts, those Western political and trade union leaders who had been relatively sanguine about Soviet intentions and capabilities changed their position. Today, a number of pessimists on both sides of the Atlantic, while recognizing that a more complex relationship exists now between the Soviets and the European labor movement, continue to sound the alarm.

United States. The Soviets have also tried to influence American labor. Until now they have been spectacularly unsuccessful. Nevertheless, they are stepping up their efforts, in the apparent belief that the crisis of capitalism and the generational change in the AFL-CIO leadership offer new opportunities. They are also seeking to take advantage of the growth of the peace/freeze movement and dissolution of the anti-communist liberal/labor coalition in the United States. For example, they are still trying to promote detente by encouraging Soviet and American trade union leader exchanges. In spite of the fact that these types of exchanges have been achieved in almost every other profession, and that senior U.S. government officials have also encouraged them in the 1970s, there have been almost no labor exchanges so far. Indeed, even Soviet efforts to send "trade union" delegations to the United States generally have failed.

Until 1977, the lack of exchanges was due to a policy decision by the Department of State not to recommend waivers of visa ineligibility (members of communist organizations must secure a waiver to enter the United States) in the case of Soviet bloc labor officials wishing to visit on trade union matters. (Bloc labor officials can and sometimes do visit the United States on tourist or other kinds of visas.) This policy was based on foreign policy considerations as well as on the attitude of the AFL-CIO regarding this question.[63]

[63]The policy and rationale were restated in a letter from Assistant Secretary for Congressional Relations Robert J. McCloskey to Representative Donald M. Fraser on

From 1977 to 1979, the "McGovern Amendment" to U.S. immigration legislation resulted in a reversal of the previous policy—during those two years labor leaders from communist nations were routinely admitted, unless two departments of the U.S. government asserted that admission of the leaders concerned would be a threat to U.S. security. In the summer of 1979, vigorous lobbying by the AFL-CIO helped result in Congressional modification of the McGovern Amendment so that it no longer automatically gave leaders of government-controlled labor fronts the waivers needed to enter the U.S. "The AFL-CIO made clear in Congressional testimony that it did not seek to prevent visits to the United States by communist officials as such or by union leaders from nations with free trade union movements who happened to be communists."[64] "Trade union" leaders from states ruled by communist parties, however, now again cannot obtain waivers to enter the United States except in special cases.

This policy has confounded the Soviets. They find it galling when they want to demonstrate that the American people, and particularly the working class, are in favor of peace, and they claim that the AFL-CIO leadership is unrepresentative of American labor. As the *Trud* correspondent in the United States put it: "It is hard to explain this phenomenon and to understand why the State Department carries out so obediently the whims of a labor union leader (George Meany) living in the past."[65]

July 6, 1976, who sought clarification of U.S. policy. The letter also indicated that the policy did not violate the agreement on the free exchange of persons embodied in CSCE (Helsinki) Final Act of 1974. McCloskey wrote that "the provision for contacts and exchanges in the labor field was raised and discussed during the CSCE negotiations. In signing the agreement, all the participants were then aware of our long-standing policy and they accepted our position against inclusion of any reference to such exchanges. . . . We do not consider that the denial of visas to the Soviet labor representatives in any way diminishes our efforts to encourage the Soviet Union to improve its performance in the area of human rights embodied in the 'Basket Three' provisions of the Final Act." This position was restated by the Carter Administration. See the Secretary of State's *Second Annual Report to the Commission on Security and Cooperation in Europe*, December 1, 1976–June 1, 1977, Special Report No. 34, June 1977, p. 21.

[64]*AFL-CIO News*, August 11, 1979, p. 7.

[65]*Trud*, December 29, 1975.

Indeed, in spite of criticism from liberal academics, State Department officials, and some unions, as well as the Soviet promise of increasing jobs from Soviet-American trade, the AFL-CIO has refused to abandon its long-time opposition to exchanges with government-controlled labor organizations, whether of the left or the right. After the Polish workers in 1980 replaced their state-controlled labor organizations with the independent *Solidarnosc* federation, the AFL-CIO felt that its policy on exchanges had been vindicated.[66]

Not only have the Soviets been unable to use most American unions to promote their concept of detente, as they have been able to do in most national centers in Europe, but they have been faced with trade unions highly critical of Soviet behavior at home and abroad. The 1976 AFL-CIO invitation to Aleksandr Solzhenitsyn was one in a series of efforts to oppose what it regarded as the major foreign policy blunder of the Nixon and Ford Administrations, the promotion of an unrealistic detente.[67]

During the Carter Administration, the AFL-CIO was strongly supportive of the President's human rights policy, but it continued to call for the West in general to stop granting gratuitous trade concessions to the communist nations.[68] With the election of Ronald Reagan in 1980, the AFL-CIO continued to attack those Western business and governmental trade policies with the Soviet bloc which labor saw as favoring corporate profits over national security and worker interests. For example, in early 1982 U.S. labor was angered by the Reagan Administration's failure to impose strong economic sanctions against Poland's Communist government after the suppression of *Solidarnosc*.[69]

[66]See James M. Shevis, "The AFL-CIO and Poland's Solidarity," *World Affairs*, Summer 1981, pp. 34–35.

[67]See Roy Godson, "American Labor's Continuing Involvement in World Affairs," *Orbis*, Spring 1975, for further details.

[68]See *Report of the AFL-CIO Executive Council to the 12th Convention*, December, 1977, pp. 204–205, 210; *Report to the 13th Convention*, November, 1979, pp. 208, 210–211.

[69]See Lane Kirkland, "A Foreign Policy With a Purpose," *The American Federationist*, April/June 1982, pp. 14–15.

Soviet efforts to use labor to influence the American economy also have been unsuccessful. Ever since the late 1940s, when the CIO purged the communists from its ranks, the Moscow-controlled Communist Party has been trying to build up communist cells in several major industries, such as steel and auto manufacturing. With rare exceptions, they have made very little headway. Nevertheless, they continue these efforts, sometimes openly and sometimes secretly.[70]

Although the Soviets and their local communist allies cannot hope to unify the American labor movement under their control, they are seeking to gain greater influence within the labor movement and to weaken the impact of the AFL-CIO on the international scene. In the 1970s American communist union officials were not in agreement on just how to do this. One school of thought, which included senior Communist Party functionaries such as Gus Hall and George Morris, believed it was hopeless to try to gain great influence in the AFL-CIO. Ironically, although they supported "world labor unity," they proposed splitting the AFL-CIO and creating a new central body of the more "progressive" AFL-CIO unions like the Steelworkers, Meat Cutters, AFSCME, and unaffiliated unions like the UAW and the United Mine Workers. In this new structure, the more "conservative," anti-communist union leadership would be weakened and the communists would have a greater chance to maneuver.

A second school, consisting for the most part of old-time communist CIO officials still active in unions like those in the United Electrical Workers (UEW), Local 1199 of the Hospital Workers, and District 65 of the Distributive Workers, wanted to increase their strength within the AFL-CIO. These officials reasoned that when George Meany departed the scene, they

---

[70]For a discussion of communist tactics and successes, particularly on the waterfront in the 1930s and 1940s, see Robert Morris, *No Wonder We Are Losing* (Plano, Texas: University of Plano Press, 1958). Morris was a senior counterintelligence officer in the New York naval district in the 1940s. See also Philip Selznik, *The Organizational Weapon* (New York: McGraw Hill, 1952). For more recent activities, see "Communist Party USA Attempts to Penetrate the Trade Union Movement," *Hearings*, Committee on Internal Security, House of Representatives, 93rd Congress, 1st Session, November 28, 1973.

would be in a better position to influence the mainstream of the labor movement if they remained a part of it. This debate within the party was won by those in favor of working inside the AFL-CIO. As Lane Kirkland succeeded to the AFL-CIO presidency in 1980, Local 1199 & District 65 merged into major AFL-CIO unions. However, there was only a marginal increase in Communist strength.

Whatever the tactics, and regardless of any lack of progress, the Soviets and their Communist Party allies have increased their efforts to gain more influence in labor. Apart from the AUCCTU, Communist Party, and KGB staff working on the United States in the Soviet Union, a "labor specialist" was openly assigned to the Soviet Embassy in Washington for the first time in 1975. Ruben A. Grigorian arrived in Washington with the title of First Secretary. Previously, he had been a Secreatary of the Metalworkers TUI and member of the AUCCTU staff. He and the *Trud* correspondent in Washington worked with the WFTU's official representative to the United States, the former UEW official Ernest de Maio, to analyze trends and opportunities.[71] Sometimes they were joined in these deliberations by the key Soviet offical in the WFTU Secretariat, Boris Averyanov. Averyanov, in his former capacity as Director of the Soviet AUCCTU International Affairs Department, had difficulty entering the United States because of the State Department's visa policy. As a WFTU official, however, he can travel at will to the United Nations in New York.

The permanent Soviet team in the United States now features First Secretary and "Labor Attache" Viktor Nikitin and Anatoly Repin, *Trud* correspondent. They are reinforced with some frequency by others, such as Boris Averyanov, and CPSU official Nikolai Mostovets, whom the *Toledo Blade* described in 1981 as an "authority on American history." Other Soviet op-

---

[71]Other diplomats and journalists also may play an important role in these deliberations. A. Mkrtchian, for example, formerly a member of the CPSU Central Committee's International Department, is the author of a book on trends in the American labor movement. Until the mid-1970s, Mkrtchian was also a senior Soviet official in Washington. Similarly, a *Tass* correspondent in New York, Nikolai Setunskiy, published a book in 1977 entitled *USA Trade Unions and Politics*.

eratives from the Communist Party, the KGB, or the AUCCTU also on occasion seek to travel to the U.S. to promote "peace and disarmament" and to support Soviet causes in the United States.

Apart from trying to arrange for labor exchanges and gaining support for Soviet policy, the Soviets are also in contact with loyal CPUSA officials working in the labor area. The CPUSA has recruited a small number of youngsters, trained them, and assigned them to tasks in support of Soviet objectives in the American labor movement. The CPUSA also participated in setting up a number of front organizations that deal with economic and political trade union issues not necessarily identified with the Communist Party—for example, the Chicago-based National Coordinating Committee for Trade Union Action and Democracy (TUAD). The ostensible major purpose of this committee is to promote more effective unions and a greater degree of democracy within unions. In fact, however, the committee is part of the Soviet bloc's effort to remove unsympathetic union leaders and gain greater influence by supporting a challenger. Another CPUSA organization supporting Soviet positions in the American labor movement is the New York-based Labor Research Association.

The major Soviet concerns are, of course, union leaders who support AFL-CIO foreign policy positions. Views on domestic legislation or collective bargaining are not the major criteria in Soviet and CPUSA decisions to support given leaders. Nor does the union official's loyalty to the Soviets cause always appear to be a decisive factor. Indeed, by supporting individuals who are not communists and whom they do not control, but who are opposed to the AFL-CIO posture, Moscow appears to be demonstrating increasing sophistication in trying to weaken "the main enemy."

The CPUSA, for example, will either join a rank-and-file challenge to a selected leader or will set up a "rank-and-file movement" on its own. In the late 1970s, for example, there were four or five "rank-and-file movements" under way, and sometimes it was difficult to distinguish the non-communist rank-and-file challenge from Soviet-financed efforts. However, although TUAD was part of Edward Sadlowski's unsuccessful challenge in the February 1977 elections of the Steelworkers, the communists have not done very well so far. Indeed, as the older generation of able U.S. communist union leaders passes from the scene (such as James Matles and Harry Bridges), very few younger American communists are stepping into their shoes. On the other hand, as the same generation of anti-communist American labor leader also leaves, the small number of active communists, though perhaps less experienced, may find it easier to maneuver and coalesce with the younger generation of trade union leaders who may not be as sensitive to the problems of working with communists.

In addition, the splintering in the 1960s and 1970s of the Democratic Party's erstwhile liberal/labor coalition also presented the Soviets with new opportunities. For most of the postwar period, labor and liberal intellectuals and politicians worked together on many economic and national security issues. From the perspective of labor, however, the liberals have been too conservative on economic issues and too weak or "soft" on foreign policy. To retain liberal support for labor's position on domestic issues, some union leaders—and particularly the younger generation—have been willing to jettison a position that for many of them has been of secondary importance, namely, a "hard line" on foreign policy. In this situation, the Soviets and their local allies have found it easier to build relationships with some sectors of the American labor movement.

Finally, the deteriorating economy in the early 1980s, coupled with the Reagan Administration's domestic budget cuts and its failure to explain adequately increasing defense expenditures resulted in a breakdown of previous barriers between "leftists" of various types and mainstream trade union officials. Many union leaders who a decade ago probably would have been much more careful about their associations, joined in anti-Reagan coalitions and demonstrations in which there was substantial participation, if not direction, by extreme leftists. Nevertheless, in spite of these domestic trends, and Soviet efforts to exploit them, the leadership of the AFL-

CIO has remained remarkably impervious to Soviet manipulation.

Third World. Unlike Western Europe, the Soviets do not have much of a trade union base in the non-Western world. But they do try to take advantage of any opportunities available to them. Sometimes they are interested in high short-term payoffs, and will try to increase their influence quickly and directly. They will, for example, take advantage of their assets, and encourage or allow their trade union clients to bring a friendly regime to power, as they tried to do in Ecuador in 1971.[72] At other times, they are willing to sacrifice short-term gains for long-term influence. For example, on occasion they have ordered the local communist party to dissolve its small trade union apparatus and merge with the main central labor body (for example, in Syria and Iraq). Such mergers are engineered either in the hope that the communists will eventually wield greater influence, or to avoid offending the government in question.

There are several prongs in Soviet labor strategy. First, a major part of their effort in the non-Western world is devoted to exploiting the considerable anti-Western sentiment in the less developed countries. Whether it is "reactionary feudalism," "neoimperialism," and Israeli "repression" in the Middle East, poverty and apartheid in Africa, or the rise of military dictatorships in Latin America, the Soviets maintain that the cause of the problem is the Western powers, and particularly the United States. This approach enables them to increase their own influence and sometimes the influence of their local allies, and correspondingly reduce that of local Western-oriented political and trade union elements opposed to such explanations. It also provides Soviet officials with the basis for coalescing with non-Western officials at international governmental and nongovernmental forums, and lays the groundwork for "labor unity."

Second, as noted earlier, the Soviet bloc has also encouraged

---

[72]James D. Theberge, *The Soviet Presence in Latin America* (New York: Crane, Russak, 1974), pp. 35–36.

Third World trade unionists to weaken the West by more direct means. Third World labor movements are encouraged to protest and sometimes impede efforts of the United States in particular to gain military base rights or secure the cooperation of non-Western governments on security issues. The Soviets and the WFTU also exhort them to follow the example of the Persian Gulf rulers, and (economic conditions permitting) to renegotiate trading arrangements and demand much higher terms from the West—which will, of course, increase inflation and affect the Western economies adversely. Third, the Soviets place great stress on "labor unity" under their influence on the national, regional, and global levels. In this essentially political approach to unifying labor under their control, the Soviets demonstrate great flexibility in their tactics.

Ideally, the Soviets strive to dominate the major trade union centers in a given country. This is not expected to happen overnight, or without great expenditures of energy and resources. First, if feasible, they establish bilateral relations with national trade union centers. Initial contact will be made either by the AUCCTU itself or, if this is not possible or desirable, by a Soviet or East European embassy official. The Soviets will suggest an exchange of delegations, friendly visits, or study trips. If these are successful, there will be an escalation of activities—joint seminars, conferences, standing committees, permanent committees, and other, permanent organizational links. Sometimes, the Soviets will seek to influence or corrupt individual labor leaders by offering them free trips, cars, money, equipment, and the like. The Soviets will also arrange for advisors to be stationed in a non-Western country; for example, the East German Gunter Goldburg was stationed in Zambia, and a Syrian communist was sent to advise the Kuwaiti unions in the 1960s. Scholarships either at the AUCCTU or East European labor schools, or sometimes at Patrice Lumumba University or the French CGT school, will be provided for local union officials. Friendly local leaders or their organizations will be offered crucial financial subsidies, and sometimes extremely close and cooperative relationships will be developed between the non-Western unions and the Soviet labor complex.

These very close labor relationships usually develop only where the governments of the day enjoy a good relationship with the Soviet Union, as the Ghanaian government did in the early 1960s, the Nigerian government in the early 1970s, or the Angolan government in the early 1980s.[73] Sometimes the Soviets will even insist that local communists dissolve their own party and trade union apparatus and enter into the legal central labor body (which the Soviets are supporting), whether the local communist parties agree or not.

There are, however, many cases in which the local government will refuse to grant direct access because of suspicions about Soviet intentions or concerns about the nonaligned image of the government. In these situations, the Soviets will work either through the WFTU or regional bodies such as ICATU and OATUU, which are ostensibly non-aligned, but which by the early 1980s were clearly tilting towards the Soviets. In the Persian Gulf, for example, the conservative rulers will not allow the Soviets legally to train officials for the incipient labor movement in places such as Bahrain. But Bahraini and other migratory workers from the region sometimes are permitted to attend WFTU-ICATU seminars. And sometimes, if even this degree of identification with the Soviet bloc would prevent individuals from attending, training is undertaken by "friendly" trade union centers (for example, in Syria, Iraq, or South Yemen) without overt identification with the Soviet bloc.[74]

One of the best illustrations of Soviet orchestration of its in-

[73]A major section of the Nigerian trade unions has been supported by the Soviet Union for a number of years. For an unusually detailed account of this operation in the late 1960s (including the names of Soviet officials, the huge sums involved, and funds that were transferred), see the articles of Arnold Beichman in the *International Herald Tribune*, January 24–25, 1970. Reference has already been made to the documents revealing the relationship between the Ghanaians and the Soviet labor complex.

[74]*Baghdad Observer*, for example, reported on May 6, 1975 that the 12th Arab two-week course held in Iraq had just graduated forty Palestinian workers from the Gulf, Egypt, Lebanon, and Libya. (The Iraqis, Syrians, and South Yemenis, for that matter, probably utilize these training sessions to increase their own influence in the region at the same time.)

ternational labor complex to gain influence in the Third World can be found in its suport of the PLO labor organization. In interviews conducted in the mid-1970s, a senior PLO official with responsibility for labor told this author that over the previous six years, approximately twenty groups of three to four Palestinians had been trained in Eastern European labor schools. This included virtually all PLO officials concerned with labor, and the interviewee himself had been trained in Eastern Europe, as well as at ICATU schools in Cairo and Damascus. In addition, the PLO labor organization (then located in southern Lebanon, Syria, and Egypt, with small branches in Western Europe to deal with Palestinian guest workers) received a subsidy every three years from the WFTU and ICATU, as well as from the PLO. (The PLO itself received money and support from a number of Communist and Arab governments.) In addition, the PLO labor organization received food, clothing, and medicines which originated in the Soviet Union and Eastern Europe. But the official claimed that few of the top PLO labor officials were Communists. Of the top seven, six had no party identification; and one, he admitted, was a Syrian Baathist. Below the top level, however, a number of the officials were either Baathists or had become communists. This pattern of the PLO labor organization working closely with the Soviets, even though most of its principal leaders were not communists, continued into the early 1980s.

It is difficult to determine with any real accuracy how much influence the Soviet international labor complex can wield in the short- and long-run. Certainly estimates will vary from place to place according to circumstances. On the one hand, many observers have concluded that organized labor does not play a significant role in the politics of non-Western countries. The wage-earning forces in most of these countries account for only a small percentage of the population (frequently no more than ten to fifteen percent), and the number of unionized workers is even smaller. The difficulties of organization are accentuated by ethnic, racial, religious, and linguistic differences, especially in Africa and many parts of Asia. Moreover, the Third World is frequently characterized by an abundant supply of unskilled labor, a high proportion of skilled migrant labor (for example, in the Persian Gulf), employer hostility, and a low level of political consciousness.

In many countries, however, organized labor has great political potential, and sometimes does play an important role. During the colonial period, the unions, sometimes directly linked with the nationalist parties and sometimes in a set of loose, short-term alliances with other groups, played a significant role in preindependence politics as well as in the independence struggle (for example, in Africa north and south of the Sahara).[75] Second, labor is one of the few organized sectors in Third World countries. In most of these societies, political institutions are weak, party structures are usually either feeble or completely nonexistent, bureaucracies are deficient, communications are poor, and there are few interest groups other than the Army and perhaps the students associations. In this situation, the trade unions represent—for all their shortcomings—a relatively coordinated and articulate pressure group. They have the capacity to make demands at the expense of other, less organized and less articulate sectors of society.

Of course, military leaders have the most effective means of political intervention, as well as the capacity to impose permanent control. But as numerous cases in the non-Western world illustrate (Goulart's Brazil in 1964, Allende's Chile in the early 1970s, the Popular Republic of the Congo after 1963, the Sudan since 1958, Ethiopia in 1973, and Benin—almost permanently since 1951) political intervention by the army and the trade unions is not mutually exclusive. As Robin Cohen has pointed out, a large-scale strike in Africa often is significant beyond the special claims of wage earners. If a confrontation is sufficiently sharp and sustained, and if it is relayed by ambitious groups, perhaps with a wider social vision, it can evolve into a fundamental challenge to a regime.[76]

[75]See, for example, the discussion of North Africa in Willard Beiling, *Modernization and African Labor, A Tunisian Case Study* (New York: Praeger, 1965); and the analysis of central and southern Africa in Robin Cohen, *Labor and Politics in Nigeria, 1945–1971* (London: Heineman, 1974), pp. 240–245.

[76]Cohen, *op. cit.*, pp. 245–252.

Moreover, unions occupy a strategic position in the economy and administration of a country. They are based in the key urban centers. If the number of unionists relative to the number of urbanized inhabitants of a country is measured (rather than comparing their number to the total population), the numerical importance of the trade unions becomes more significant. The government and public corporations also invariably are the most important employers in numerical terms (in many African countries, the government employs about half the wage-earning population), so that any major industrial action has at least implicit political consequences. When these actions take place in strategic public sectors, such as the railways, docks, and post and telegraph, the unions have even greater political leverage.[77]

The unions, despite their small numbers, also have considerable propaganda strength and can influence the opinions of a sizeable number of their own members, as well as people outside the union structure. This influence derives from the relatively elevated status of the wage earners and their location in the process of political socialization and communication. Workers may migrate to the city, where they are socialized; and when they return to the countryside, even if only for brief periods of time, they are listened to by their relatives and friends in the rural areas.[78] Finally, the living circumstances of the worker frequently dispose him or her to hold distinct social attitudes and to take collective action. The worker has been wrenched away from many of the traditional social controls, and often is the victim of overcrowded cities with poor housing and sanitation, incompetent police forces, and sometimes even a breakdown in the network of food distribution. In these circumstances, labor movements can become the focus of enormous discontent.

These and other factors explain the opportunities and the predisposition of the unions to play an important political role. In spite of the fact that post-independence political parties are

---

[77] *Ibid.*

[78] See, for example, *ibid.*, *passim;* and John H. Magill, *Labor Unions and Political Socialization, A Case Study of Bolivian Workers* (New York: Praeger, 1974).

able to effect a measure of control over most interest groups, the ease with which they are overthrown, usually by the military, indicates that the political process in the first years of independence is complex. Parties are rarely strong in and of themselves, and decisions are made as a result of bargaining with major groups both inside and outside the party. Sometimes the ruling party has been able to subordinate the unions under its control (e.g., Nyerere's Tanzania, Nkrumah's Ghana, and Sekou Touré's Guinea); at other times, there was a partnership (e.g., Kenyatta's Kenya, Bourguiba's Tunisia in the 1960s, Houphouet-Boigny's Ivory Coast); and at other times, the unions were aligned with important opposition parties (e.g., Morocco, Botswana, and Albert Margai's Sierra Leone in the 1960s).

Even under military rule, unions can have considerable political leverage. An army on its road to political power, or once it has assumed power, may attempt to include in its base a wider section of the population; and the unions, which are not part of the old order, provide a useful base of legitimacy. A good example of this strategy would be Major N'Gouabi's Congo-Brazzaville after 1969. In other instances, army factions bid for the support of various institutions after a coup, as in the case of the "insecure" army in the Sudan since 1958.[79] In Latin America, military rulers have sometimes felt it necessary to seek the cooperation of one part of the labor movement in order to contain what they regard as a more dangerous threat to their role from another part. For example, in Peru (1969-71) and Honduras (1975-76), the military allied with the communist-led unions against the non-communists.

Yet another pattern emerges in the case of Benin. There the country is divided into roughly three regional power blocs, and it is essential for the power contestants, whether military or civilian, to control the capital of Cotonou. Through the early 1970s, no political faction of note was able to maintain Cotonou without the support of the unions.[80]

[79]Cohen, *op. cit.*, pp. 252–260.
[80]*Ibid.*

No doubt other patterns and relationships between labor and the governments of the Third World will emerge in the future; but under these circumstances, Soviet influence in the labor movement of Third World countries becomes significant. Although the Soviets began to train cadres for work in these areas even during the colonial period, they did not mount a major effort until the late 1950s. As was discussed above, they do not expect their efforts over the last twenty years to result in a monopoly of power for Moscow-oriented political groups. The Kremlin has already reaped some benefits, however, and continues to look at the Third World in long-range terms.

Africa. In Africa, the Soviets have had some success which has yielded political benefits. But they have also suffered setbacks. Until recently, at least, Moscow has concentrated on trying to build up politically reliable cadres in the top echelons of the unions, rather than attempting to build mass organizations which could serve the bread-and-butter interests of the workers.

In Northern Africa, Soviet gains have been marginal. The communist parties remain small and, for the most part, underground organizations. Even where the Soviets have arranged training programs and exchanged delegations and communiques, the impact has been minor. The best example of this is Morocco, where in spite of a fairly cooperative relationship with the head of the Union Marocain du Travail (UMT), which is a center of opposition to the King, very few Moroccan union leaders have become communist. Nor are they enamored with the Soviet regime, although by and large they have had little contact with, and are not particularly well disposed toward, the West.[81] In Tunisia, the Soviets have had even less success. It is quite possible, however, that in Algeria and Libya, where the governments have been more friendly with the Soviet Union (and where the unions usually follow the government line), the Soviets may have made more headway.

In Sub-Saharan Africa, there is a similar pattern of Soviet

[81]Interviews with UMT officials, June 1976.

concentration on the higher levels of union leadership. Most labor movements in this area are government-controlled. Consequently, during periods when a given government is very friendly with the Soviet Union, that government often forces the trade unions to follow the same line. Their top leadership is trained by Moscow, the national centers are affiliated to the WFTU, and they cooperate with the Soviets in international forums. This pattern prevailed in Somalia and in Congo-Brazzaville in the mid-1970s, and in Angola and Mozambique in the early 1980s.

A particularly striking example of the imposition of communist leadership on a labor movement occurred in Ethiopia. In the spring of 1974, the relatively free and Western-oriented Confederation of Ethiopian Trade Unions (CELU) succeeded in organinzing a general strike, which together with student disruptions was a major factor in leading to the overthrow of Emperor Haile Selassie. After the CELU leadership claimed the new military regime was practically as oppressive as the Emperor's government, the organization was closed down, only to be reborn a few months later. The new leaders had no previous CELU background. Instead, they had been selected by the Soviet Embassy for training in Moscow. After taking over CELU, they adopted Moscow's political line; and in a June 1975 statement, claimed that CELU previously had been supporting imperialism and the policies of the ICFTU and the AFL-CIO, instead of the progressive line of the WFTU. As a result, it was necessary to sever all relations with the AFL-CIO and establish relations with "all progressive organizations of the broad masses."

The strength of loyalty to communism and to the U.S.S.R. among the union leadership in these cases is not easy to determine. As the case of post-Nkrumah Ghana reveals, once pressure from the government ceases, an anti-Soviet leadership can come to the fore quite easily. Alternatively, if a government shifts to an anti-Soviet foreign policy stance, it can actively move to depose the pro-Soviet union leadership. This happened in the Sudan, where a large Communist Party and trade union movement loyal to Moscow had been built up, only to be literally wiped out by a new military regime. A similar reversal is always a possibility in Ethiopia. In any event, the Soviets' long-term approach of training and wooing cadres of leaders provides them with capable personnel in instances where pro-Soviet regimes seek pro-communist trade unionists to place in power.

In other areas of sub-Saharan Africa, where governments have not been aligned with the U.S.S.R., the benefits of Soviet training and support for friendly labor leaders are slower to appear. The Soviet program in Nigeria, mentioned previously, has continued into the early 1980s, when the Nigerian Labor Congress expanded its exchanges of delegations with Soviet-bloc nations, and with the AUCCTU itself. In the fall of 1980 the Nigerians sent three labor leaders to the ten-month course at the Higher Trade Union School in Moscow, and by 1981 sixty Nigerian trade unionists were in training in the Soviet bloc as a whole. By 1982 the Nigerian government was concerned about the pro-Soviet orientation of the Nigerian Labor Congress. In Senegal and the Ivory Coast, Soviet efforts to recruit labor have been much less successful than in Nigeria, where the communists are virtually frozen out of the labor movement. In tightly controlled regimes, such as Zaire, legal in-country Soviet activity is not permitted.

In Southern Africa, the Soviets long-term strategy has already paid off in the former Portugese colonies, and the Soviets have been preparing for an influential role in post-apartheid South Africa. In Angola and Mozambique, they had for years been supporting and training the MPLA and FRELIMO military and trade union leaders who eventually emerged as the victorious elements. As a result, the new leaders of the labor movement in these areas were basically pro-Soviet, and Moscow and the WFTU have continued to provide them with subsidies, training, and the like.[82]

In South Africa, the Soviets cannot operate legally, and the underground organizations they support (the South African

[82]See, for example, *Flashes*, February 25, 1976, and *Flashes*, September 10, 1976, for a joint UNTA and WFTU communique.

Communist Party, the African National Congress, and SACTU, the South African Confederation of Trade Unions) have been able to exert little influence on the labor situation during the 1970s and early 1980s. In the 1950s and 1960s, the Communists had gained major influence in the SACTU, which was then operating openly. During the 1960s government repression of the SACTU increased to the point that in 1967 the organization went underground. The covert SACTU is pro-Soviet. It is affiliated to the WFTU and receives material support from the body.[83]

In a postapartheid South Africa the Soviets—as a result of their training and support of South African refugees and undergound organizations—will have trained leaders who can step into the breach. As they did in the 1970s in Portugal, Spain, and Ethiopia, pro-Soviet forces may well emerge from obscurity to control strategic sectors of the society—unless, of course, there is an alternative leadership unmarked by association with the current regime. In Botswana, Lesotho, and Swaziland, however, the Soviets appear to have little influence either through contacts, training, or by gaining a substantial base in the leadership of the labor movement.

Middle East. Moscow's influence in the labor movement in the Middle East varies from country to country. In countries where the regime is friendly to the Soviet Union, there is a close cooperative relationship between the Soviet international labor complex and local labor organizations. This has been true especially in Iraq, South Yemen, and Syria. As was discussed earlier, the Soviets cooperate on propaganda and training both in these countries and, through them, in the region as a whole. As the Arab world, and particularly the Persian Gulf states, industrializes, this cooperation may be very important indeed, especially as there is almost no countervailing anti-Soviet trade union presence in the area.

Soviet influence in Egypt, however, where the unions until Nasser's time fostered a tradition of independence, has not been

[83]Roy Godson, "Black Labor as a Swing Factor in South Africa's Evolution," in Richard Bissel and Chester Crocker, eds., *South Africa Into the 1980s*, (Boulder, Col.: Westview Press, 1979).

as extensive as might be thought. In spite of close association with and training by the bloc for twenty years, pro-Soviet forces did not become dominant either in the Egyptian Federation of Labor (EFL) or in the Egyptian-run ICATU during the period when Egyptian-Soviet relations were close. This lack of progress was not for lack of Soviet effort. In both the EFL and ICATU, the Soviets tried to help friendly Arabs become dominant. Under the encouragement of the Sadat regime, however, non-communist leaders resisted; and in ICATU, the Egyptians were able to mobilize support from the Moroccan, Tunisian, and Lebanese labor movements to resist Soviet, Syrian, and Libyan efforts to take over in the early 1970s. There is still considerable pro-Soviet sentiment in certain Egyptian trade-union circles, however, and it remains to be seen what strength these groups may obtain in Egyptian labor in the post-Sadat era.

Asia. In Southern and Southeast Asia, the Soviets not only have to contend with governments that are wary of their influence, but also with Bejing-oriented communists. With the exception of India, Vietnam, Laos, and the Philippines, the Soviets have little influence in trade union circles in the area. The Kremlin is, however, stepping up its Asian efforts. The strategy focuses on exchanges of delegations and the training of a small number of friendly Asians both in the Soviet Union and Eastern Europe, and locally through the WFTU and its Indian affiliate, AITUC. As already noted, however, very few Asian labor organizations so far have been willing to affiliate with the WFTU, and the Soviets have not been able to work through a regional labor body. Nevertheless, the WFTU is organizing regional education conferences, establishing a "permanent representation" in the area, and promoting "various measures and activities aimed at holding a United Trade Union Conference."

The Soviets have mounted major programs, and have made major gains, in the South Pacific. Communists of various outlooks for many years have had significant influence in the labor movements of Australia and New Zealand. In the early 1980s they influenced or controlled about one-fifth of Australia's organized workers. "Eurocommunists" controlled the metalworkers—Australia's single largest union—while Moscow-line Communists were strong in the building trades. In New Zealand communist influence is possibly even stronger. Numerous trade union leaders are members of the Moscow-line Socialist Unity Party, including senior officials of the New Zealand Federation of Labor. Top Federation leaders often take pro-Soviet positions on such foreign policy issues as disarmament, Chile, Poland, and Afghanistan.

Communist strength in Australia and New Zealand is carefully nurtured by the U.S.S.R. Numerous labor leaders are invited to the U.S.S.R. and Eastern European countries every year. For example, in the late 1970s and early 1980s six groups of twenty persons from the Australian unions were brought to Moscow annually for a six-week course on "The Role of Trade Unions in a Socialist Society."

The Soviets, in collaboration with trade union contacts in Australia and New Zealand, are increasing communist influence among the small trade unions in the various islands of the South Pacific. The main vehicle for this effort has been a series of regional labor conferences in the South Pacific, sponsored by several Australian or New Zealand communist labor leaders. For example, in November 1979 the WFTU and Australian Communists sponsored a "South Pacific-Asian Trade Union Unity Conference," held in Sydney, and in May of 1981 there was a "Pacific Trade-Union Forum" in Vanuatu. At these conferences the major themes include making the South Pacific a nuclear-free zone and eliminating all foreign military bases from the area. (The only nuclear installations and military bases in the South Pacific are of course Western, not Soviet).

Latin America and the Caribbean. In Central and South America and the Caribbean, the Soviets and the Cubans also stepped up their efforts in the 1970s, taking advantage of recent political trends. One is rapid industrialization, which is taking place in many parts of the region. The ensuing instability and turmoil, both in urban and rural areas, creates unfulfilled expectations as well as misery and discontent, which have often been fertile ground for communist agitation. The growth of nationalism and anti-Americanism is another factor which facilitates communist penetration. In this atmosphere, it is relatively easy for the Soviets and their local allies to build an "anti-American imperialist" front.

A third factor which may have helped pro-Soviet elements has been the increase in the number and severity of right-wing dictatorships in the region. Maintaining power by repressing those institutions that stand in their way, and frequently by brutal suppression, these authoritarian governments often help the Soviet-backed minorities to rally all those opposed to the regime, propose far-reaching "democratic" reforms, ally themselves with other parties and trade unionists (even those that are anti-communist), and eventually assume control of the anti-regime coalition. Flaunting their so-called anti-dictatorial reputation as well as the organizations they have created, the communists then have posed as the champions of democracy.

This scenario explains how the Sandinistas, an inconsequential Marxist splinter group in the early 1970s, were able to seize the political initiative in 1978, spearhead military effort against the Somoza dictatorship, and then replace Somoza with an increasingly totalitarian Marxist-Leninist regime. With the unification of several Marxist-Leninist guerilla bands in El Salvador in 1980, and the formation of a "Democratic Revolutionary Front" under their control, the communist left has unified communists and non-communists, and has mounted a similar challenge in El Salvador.

Capitalizing on these favorable political trends, the Soviets have brought their international apparatus to bear on the region. They have also been able to take advantage of Cuba's proclaimed status as a "nonaligned," Third World nation, and the Cuban Communist Party and "trade unions" are playing a major role in Soviet efforts.

Because Latin America is viewed as a more advanced area, with an urban and to some extent rural proletariat (unlike Africa and Asia), the Soviets have concentrated on building up communist parties and trade union organizations. In many countries, there is a daily Party or trade union newspaper. The communist union officials can also call on the services of communist labor lawyers; and in a number of countries, the communists offer a variety of medical, welfare, and trade union services to workers.[84] The WFTU, CPUSTAL, and local communist unions also have been organizing an increasing number of training seminars, in addition to the financing and training efforts in Cuba and the Soviet bloc.

So far, however, Moscow has not been able to wield great influence in the labor movement in the region. Communist-controlled unions remained small and weak, though in the late 1970s they became significant factors in Colombia, the Dominican Republic, Ecuador, Honduras, and Panama. Until the late 1970s most of them were affiliated with CPUSTAL, which was also very weak. Some twenty two communist Confederations have now affiliated openly with the WFTU.

The Soviets, and particularly the Cubans, have increased their overall labor activities in the past few years. In several places, for example in Colombia and Honduras, Soviet- and Cuban-supported communists have succeeded in gaining control of important unions. In Nicaragua, Guyana, and other places, they also are becoming increasingly influential. Whether Moscow will be able to continue to capitalize on trends in this and other parts of the world will depend on a number of factors, including the conclusions drawn by policymakers in the democratic world.

Conclusion

Although some argue that the Kremlin has lost interest in the use of organized labor in its global strategy, clearly this is not the case. True, the Soviets have acquired superpower status and place greater emphasis on state-to-state relations and traditional instruments of statecraft than ever before. But they

---

[84]Reliable, detailed information on communist labor activities is difficult to come by. One of the few attempts to gather information can be found in *Anti-Democratic Labor Activities in Latin America, Report of an Informal Survey*, Georgetown University International Labor Program, Washington, D. C., Summer 1976.

are still employing a transnational strategy—they are attempting to influence both governments and important nongovernmental sectors throughout the world. For them the labor instrument, like the military instrument, is one of the major means of affecting political conditions in the non-communist world. Soviet leaders and analysts stress the importance of the subject; and past Soviet practice indicates that labor has been seen and used as a political tool. Today, the Kremlin continues to devote considerable attention, resources, and manpower to weakening Western influence and gaining control of the labor sector abroad.

The full significance of labor in Soviet strategy, however, is not always immediately apparent. Viewed in isolation, organized labor in the non-communist world, even under Soviet influence, is not necessarily important. The labor movement, however, can affect public policy, the power of a government to rule, and even the continued existence of a political system. Interacting with political parties, the military, and other important actors, control of the labor movement is one of the important factors affecting the outcome of the struggle for power in many countries.

Although labor is important and the Soviets are aware of this, their efforts so far have not enabled them to acquire complete control of the trade union movement in most of the non-communist world. In the developed areas, which the Soviets claim to see as the most promising, they have had only mixed success at best. In the United States, they have almost no influence in the labor movement. But they have become far more sophisticated. They are supporting coalitions designed to weaken the anti-totalitarian leadership of the AFL-CIO, rather than only assisting communists in gaining influential positions. If they are even partially successful, they will weaken the AFL-CIO as a counterweight to their efforts in various parts of the world, and they will also weaken the pro-defense coalition in Washington, of which the AFL-CIO is an important part.

On the whole, in Northern Europe, West Germany, Britain, and the Benelux countries, they have not been able to secure major influence in the unions, although they have been able to use labor in these countries to promote the Soviet concept of detente, and to reduce European support for NATO decisions. In Southern or Latin Europe, however, they have been the beneficiaries of communist control of major sections of the labor movement. For the moment, however, anti-communist democratic socialist parties are ascendant, and most of the southern European communist parties are neither as strong nor as responsive to Soviet direction as Moscow would wish. If, however, these communist parties should come to dominate the labor movement and the Soviets remain influential, the entire political orientation of the area might very well shift. Labor would not only be available to promote Soviet propaganda interests, but it would probably also become an effective part of a major effort to detach Southern Europe from the Western alliance, and enable the communist parties to secure a monopoly of political power.

In the less developed areas, where they see targets of opportunity, the Soviets and their local allies generally have not obtained significant results. Usually, where the labor movement has been almost completely trained and/or financed by the Soviet labor complex, this has come as a result of the local government's close ties to the Soviet bloc. When such governmental ties deteriorate, the close relationship between the Soviets and the local labor movement tends to decline accordingly. As the years pass, however, the Soviets are training and financing many thousands of non-Western union officials. While their ability to influence non-Westerners by financing them may not extend very far beyond the last payment, the large number of Soviet bloc-trained union officials may give them important assets in the future. At a minimum, these labor leaders will not be pro-Western, and many of them will be pro-Soviet. Many of them can be counted on to assist the Soviets in weakening Western security interests and possibly also to assist local communist interests.

In some areas, such as parts of Latin America, Africa, and Asia, Western trade unionists, principally American, are training and supporting some local union leaders. In other areas, there is no Western trade union presence at all. In two crucial places, the Persian Gulf and South Africa, the only significant training and support in the labor area throughout the 1970s came from the Soviet bloc. As the Persian Gulf industrializes the Soviets may find themselves in an increasingly influential position. The Soviets also are clearly aiming for a post-apartheid South Africa with few Western-oriented black trade union leaders in a large black industrial work force.[85]

Thus, while the Soviets have not been able to gain control of the labor movement in most places, they are continuing to expand their control of this strategically important sector. They already have reaped some benefits from their efforts; and over the long run, they may be able to acquire an influential base of support in a number of countries. If the West does not provide assistance to non-communist trade unions which request it, the Soviets will have the entire field to themselves. Western specialists need to know much more about organized labor and the circumstances under which Soviet efforts are and are not effective. Only then can a meaningful strategy be developed to counter Soviet efforts, and enhance genuinely democratic values throughout the world.

[85]See *The AFL-CIO Free Trade Union News*, May, 1982, pp. 4–5. On the general situation of black labor in South Africa, and recommendations for Western action in support of black trade unions there, see Roy Godson, "Black Labor As a Swing Factor in South Africa's Evolution," *op. cit.*

Appendix

Major Actors in the International Labor Movement

Global Internationals

WFTU   *World Federation of Trade Unions.* Soviet-
            dominated. Created in 1945. Originally the
            British TUC, the American CIO, and other
            non-communist national centers were
            affiliated, but broke away in 1948–49.

WCL   *World Confederation of Labor.* Christian-
            oriented. Originally established in 1920 as
            International Federation of Christian Trade
            Unions. Changed its name in 1968.

ICFTU   *International Confederation of Free Trade
            Unions.* Now predominantly social democratic.
            Created in 1949 by the AFL-CIO and non-
            communist European national centers which
            broke with the WFTU. The AFL-CIO
            withdrew in 1969, but reaffiliated in 1982.

Industrial Internationals

TUIs   *Trade Union Internationals.* Soviet-dominated. Attached to WFTU.

TIs   *Trade Internationals.* Attached to WCL.

ITS   *International Trade Secretariats.* Independent, but on close terms with the ICFTU. About half of the AFL-CIO internationals are affiliated with their respective secretariats.

Regional Internationals

ICATU   *International Confederation of Arab Trade Unions.* Officially nonaligned. Created by the Egyptians in 1956.

AATUF   *All-African Trade Union Federation.* Officially nonaligned. Created by the "Casablanca Group" in 1961, and dissolved in 1976.

OATUU   *Organization of African Trade Union Unity.* Officially nonaligned. Created in 1973 under the aegis of the Organization of African Unity (OAU).

CPUSTAL   *Permanent Committee for Labor Unity in Latin America.* Moscow-oriented. Created originally as CUTAL in 1962.

ETUC   *European Trade Union Confederation.* Created in 1973 by ICFTU affiliates, stressing the common bonds of all European unions.

National Centers

AUCCTU   *All-Union Central Council of Trade Unions.* Soviet Union, affiliated with WFTU.

CGT   *General Confederation of Labor.* France, communist-controlled, affiliated with WFTU.

CGT-FO   *"Force Ouvrière."* France, non-communist, affiliated with the ICFTU and the ETUC.

CFTD   *French Confederation of Democratic Trade Unions.* Formerly Christian, affiliated with WCL and ETUC.

CGIL   *Italian Confederation of Labor.* Communist-controlled, and affiliated with the ETUC.

CISL   *Italian Confederation of Trade Unions.* Christian, affiliated with the ICFTU and ETUC.

UIL   *Italian Union of Labor.* Socialist and social democratic, affiliated with the ICFTU and ETUC.

TUC   *Trades Union Congress.* British, primarily Socialist non-communist, affiliated with the ICFTU and ETUC.

DGB   *West German Trade Union Federation.* Primarily social democratic, affiliated with the ICFTU and the ETUC.

AFL-CIO   *American Federation of Labor-Congress of Industrial Organizations.* Reaffiliated with the ICFTU.

National Strategy Information Center, Inc.

PUBLICATIONS

Joyce E. Larson, Editor
William C. Bodie, Editor

STRATEGY PAPERS

Labor in Soviet Global Strategy by Roy Godson, May 1984

The Soviet Control Structure: Capabilities for Wartime Survival by Harriet Fast Scott and William F. Scott, September 1983

Strategic Weapons: An Introduction by Norman Polmar, October 1975. Revised edition, June 1982

Conventional War and Escalation: The Soviet View by Joseph D. Douglass, Jr. and Amoretta M. Hoeber, November 1981

Soviet Perceptions of Military Doctrine and Military Power: The Interaction of Theory and Practice by John J. Dziak, June 1981

How Little is Enough? SALT and Security in the Long Run by Francis P. Hoeber, January 1981

Raw Material Supply in a Multipolar World by Yuan-li Wu, October 1973. Revised edition, October 1979

India: Emergent Power? by Stephen P. Cohen and Richard L. Park, June 1978

The Kremlin and Labor: A Study in National Security Policy by Roy Godson, November 1977

The Evolution of Soviet Security Strategy 1965-1975 by Avigdor Haselkorn, November 1977

The Geopolitics of the Nuclear Era by Colin S. Gray, September 1977

The Sino-Soviet Confrontation: Implications for the Future by Harold C. Hinton, September 1976 (Out of print)

Food, Foreign Policy, and Raw Materials Cartels by William Schneider, Jr., February 1976

Soviet Sources of Military Doctrine and Strategy by William F. Scott, July 1975

Detente: Promises and Pitfalls by Gerald L. Steibel, March 1975 (Out of print)

Oil, Politics and Sea Power: The Indian Ocean Vortex by Ian W. A. C. Adie, December 1974 (Out of print)

The Soviet Presence in Latin America by James D. Theberge, June 1974

The Horn of Africa by J. Bowyer Bell, Jr., December 1973

Research and Development and the Prospects for International Security by Frederick Seitz and Rodney W. Nichols, December 1973

99

AGENDA PAPERS

The China Sea: The American Stake in its Future by Harold C. Hinton, January 1981

NATO, Turkey, and the Southern Flank: A Mideastern Perspective by Ihsan Gürkan, March 1980 (Out of Print)

The Soviet Threat to NATO's Northern Flank by Marian K. Leighton, November 1979

Does Defense Beggar Welfare? Myths Versus Realities by James L. Clayton, June 1979 (Out of print)

Naval Race or Arms Control in the Indian Ocean? (Some Problems in Negotiating Naval Limitations) by Alvin J. Cottrell and Walter F. Hahn, September 1978 (Out of print)

Power Projection: A Net Assessment of U.S. and Soviet Capabilities by W. Scott Thompson, April 1978

Understanding the Soviet Military Threat: How CIA Estimates Went Astray by William T. Lee, February 1977 (Out of print)

Toward a New Defense for NATO: The Case for Tactical Nuclear Weapons, July 1976 (Out of print)

Seven Tracks to Peace in the Middle East by Frank R. Barnett, April 1975

Arms Treaties with Moscow: Unequal Terms Unevenly Applied? by Donald G. Brennan, April 1975 (Out of print)

Toward a U.S. Energy Policy by Klaus Knorr, March 1975 (Out of print)

Can We Avert Economic Warfare in Raw Materials? US Agriculture as a Blue Chip by William Schneider, Jr., July 1974 (Out of print)

BOOKS

On the Brink: Defense, Deficits, and Welfare Spending by James L. Clayton, November 1983

U.S. International Broadcasting and National Security by James L. Tyson, November 1983

Arms, Men, and Military Budgets: Issues for Fiscal Year 1981 by Francis P. Hoeber, William Schneider, Jr., Norman Polmar, and Ray Bessette, May 1980

Arms, Men, and Military Budgets: Issues for Fiscal Year 1979 by Francis P. Hoeber, David B. Kassing, and William Schneider, Jr., February 1978

Arms, Men, and Military Budgets: Issues for Fiscal Year 1978 edited by Francis P. Hoeber and William Schneider, Jr., May 1977

Arms, Men, and Military Budgets: Issues for Fiscal Year 1977 edited by William Schneider, Jr. and Francis P. Hoeber, May 1976

Intelligence Requirements for the 1980s: Clandestine Collection (Volume V of a Series) edited by Roy Godson, November 1982

Intelligence Requirements for the 1980s: Covert Action (Volume IV of a Series) edited by Roy Godson, September 1981

Intelligence Requirements for the 1980s: Counterintelligence (Volume III of a Series) edited by Roy Godson, January 1981

Intelligence Requirements for the 1980s: Analysis and Estimates (Volume II of a Series) edited by Roy Godson, June 1980

Intelligence Requirements for the 1980s: Elements of Intelligence (Volume I of a Series) edited by Roy Godson, October 1979. Revised edition, October 1983

The Soviet View of U.S. Strategic Doctrine by Jonathan Samuel Lockwood, April 1983

Strategic Military Surprise: Incentives and Opportunities edited by Klaus Knorr and Patrick Morgan, January 1983

National Security Affairs: Theoretical Perspectives and Contemporary Issues edited by B. Thomas Trout and James E. Harf, October 1982

False Science: Underestimating the Soviet Arms Buildup by Steven Rosefielde, July 1982

Our Changing Geopolitical Premises by Thomas P. Rona, January 1982

Strategic Minerals: A Resource Crisis published by the Council on Economics and National Security (an NSIC Project), December 1981

U.S. Policy and Low-Intensity Conflict: Potentials for Military Struggles in the 1980s edited by Sam C. Sarkesian and William L. Scully, June 1981

New Foundations for Asian and Pacific Security edited by Joyce E. Larson, September 1980

The Fateful Ends and Shades of SALT: Past . . . Present . . . And Yet to Come? by Paul H. Nitze, James E. Dougherty, and Francis X. Kane, March 1979

Strategic Options for the Early Eighties: What Can Be Done? edited by William R. Van Cleave and W. Scott Thompson, February 1979

Oil, Divestiture and National Security edited by Frank N. Trager, December 1976 (Out of print)

Indian Ocean Naval Limitations: Regional Issues and Global Implications by Alvin J. Cottrell and Walter F. Hahn, April 1976

The Intelligent Layperson's Guide to the Nuclear Freeze and Peace Debate by Joyce E. Larson and William C. Bodie, March 1983

War and Peace: Soviet Russia Speaks edited by Albert L. Weeks and William C. Bodie, with an essay by Frank R. Barnett, March 1983

The National Strategy Information Center is a non-partisan tax-exempt institution organized in 1962 to conduct educational programs in international security affairs.

The Center espouses no political causes. Its Directors and Officers represent a wide spectrum of responsible political opinion from liberal to conservative. What unites them, however, is the conviction that neither isolationism nor pacifism can provide realistic solutions to the challenge of 20th century totalitarianism.

NSIC exists to encourage civil-military partnership on the grounds that, in a democracy, informed public opinion is necessary to a viable U.S. defense system capable of protecting the nation's vital interests and assisting other free nations which aspire to independence and self-fulfillment.